Also in the Star to Cell series by Fabien Maman

Book I : *The Role of Music in the Twenty-First Century*

Book II: *Raising Human Frequencies: The Way of Chi and the Subtle Bodies*

Book III: *The Body as a Harp: Sound and Acupuncture*

From Star to Cell:
A Sound Structure for the Twenty-First Century

Book IV

Healing with Sound, Color and Movement

Nine Evolutionary Healing Techniques

Fabien Maman

Healing with Sound, Color and Movement

Nine Evolutionary Healing Techniques

Fabien Maman

Published by:

Tama-Dõ Press
2060 Las Flores Canyon
Malibu, CA 90265
800.615.3675
info@tama-do.com
www.tamado.com

Reprint: 2005

Cover Illustration by Hilary Pearson
Typography and Graphic Design by David Haefeli and Coloria S à r.l.
Illustrations by Jean-Luc Haldimann of Coloria S à r.l.
Copy Editing by Cynthia Reber Maman and Susan Klopman
Sefirotic Tree Technique transcribed by Fran Higgins
Library of Congress Catalog Card number 97-90566
Maman, Fabien
Printed in Poland by Morpol

ISBN 0-9657714-3-1

Disclaimer

The healing techniques described in this book are not intended as a substitute for regular medical attention. In addition, Fabien Maman, Tama-Dõ Press and the Academy of Sound, Color and Movement cannot be held responsible for the results of the use of these methods when practiced without proper training as taught by the Academy of Sound, Color and Movement.

For Jacques Duponchelle...

With Gratitude

Without the help of Cynthia Reber Maman this book would not have been written. The entire series of books, *From Star to Cell: A Sound Structure for the Twenty-First Century*, represents hundreds of teaching cassette tapes from many different countries which Cynthia transcribed and worked with me to put into book form. It was truly a joint effort as well as a monumental task of commitment, dedication and love.

Acknowledgements

I would like to thank all of the students of the Academy of Sound, Color and Movement and especially Fran Higgins for her transcription of the Sefirotic Tree healing technique, Mary Pout and Hilary Pearson for computer charts and artwork, Patricia Janus for her "guided" support and color research, Dr. Patrick Camus for the generous sharing of his color research as well as his home when we needed a place to write, and Jeff Chitourus who said early on that "this stuff should be in a book" and has offered support and advice all along the way. A special thanks to Christina Ross for her continuous enthusiasm and willingness be of service no matter what the task and to Harry and Mary Reber who offered their hospitality and support throughout the project.

Thanks also to David, Frédéric and Jean-Luc of Coloria, of Switzerland, who supplied their gifts for computer graphics and to Susan Klopman for her editing skills. I am also grateful to Dr. Rene Gandolfi of Paris for his early and immediate recognition of the value of this work and for his continual friendship and support. Finally, my deep appreciation to the source of the inspiration I have received in my work and in my life.

Contents

Preface to the Series
From Star to Cell: A Sound Structure for the Twenty-First Century

The series of books, *From Star to Cell: A Sound Structure for the Twenty-First Century,* represents my nearly twenty years of research with energy including sound, color, chi movement and acupuncture.

As I learned the laws of the vibrational world in the body through the practices of acupuncture and Aikido I became more tuned to the invisible worlds of the subtle bodies and the vibrational frequencies of chi movement, sound and color. I began to sense the design of a subtle energetic structure based on acupuncture and my work in laboratory with cells and sound (shown in Book I), which links human beings through resonance to nature and the cosmos.

This living structure is based on the laws of acupuncture in the physical body and continues through the five elements of nature to the subtle bodies and even to the vibrational messages of stars and planets. Through the frequencies of the subtle bodies, we can find a resonance with the highest energetic information. The acupuncture base in the body ensures that all information can be integrated physically through the correct channels, or acupuncture meridians.

From this structure I developed several techniques which utilize the vibrational powers of sound, color and movement to heal and balance the physical and subtle bodies. These techniques, many of which can also be used for self-healing, will perhaps be best understood if they are read after the foundation has been set by the previous three books in this series.

Book I offers the photographic results of my experiments with human cells and sound and introduces the theories of music that inspired the development of the sound healing techniques. Book II is devoted to the investigation into the nature of our subtle anatomy and chi, the energetic essence that runs through and links the physical and subtle bodies. Book III explores the acupuncture and sound foundation of the healing techniques which are offered in this, the fourth book of the series.

I offer this book to healers and self-healers alike as an introduction to the beauty and therapeutic potential of the vibrational tools of sound, color and movement.

Fabien Maman
Autumn, 1997
Domaine des Courmettes
France

Introduction

The Art of Healing

Healing should be an artistic synthesis of beauty, harmony and inspiration. Healing is an expression of love. The soul must be nourished and given hope for the body to heal. If you seek healing for yourself, you must establish communication with your higher self, just as your body talks to you by telling you where it needs attention. You are the medium between your body and your higher self.

You are not only your body and you are not only your higher self. Then who are you? Perhaps by going through the healing process you will answer this eternal question. As the anonymous monk said centuries ago, "I am not the sky. And I am not the earth. I am the wind. Who can hurt the wind?"

The healer can offer a flexible mirror so that the different realms of resonance can be awakened in each human being. The art of healing is to create a resonance between the higher self and the body. This resonance initiates recognition, understanding, knowledge, restoration, recentering and finally healing.

Healing Resonance

In everyday life there are many circumstances which can activate a resonance with higher aspects of yourself such meeting an inspiring person, being moved by the beauty of an unusual landscape, a sunset or the blue of the Mediterranean sea, or by listening to beautiful music, to the wind in the forest, or to the song of a bird.

Love, music and nature offer the most sublime and uplifting possibilities of resonance and when this resonance is blocked we suffer; we are out of balance with the higher aspects of ourselves. Seeking elevated experiences and allowing yourself to be touched and moved by the beauty in life will certainly start the natural process of your own healing and evolution. Your task is to continue this process and to help others evolve through resonance with the finer vibratory gifts of life.

In the future, human abilities for healing energetically will be highly developed.[1] In the meantime, a strong healing resonance can be offered through the vibration of music, played with the pure sound of acoustic instruments and the human voice. Acoustic instruments and the human voice are the only tools which offer the entire range of overtone.[2]

There is a strong healing power in the overtones of a sound. Because of the property of anti-matter of the overtone, a delicate weightless quality is brought by overtones to our own vibration; we feel light like an angel. This is what the right kind of music can offer. People love music because it literally makes them feel lighter. As Schopenauer has said, "Music seems to whisper in our ear, "Listen to me, I can transform you."

Matter is naturally heavy, anti-matter is light. The same parallel can be seen between the physical body and the subtle bodies. There is a natural resonance between the physical body and the subtle bodies. The matter of the body is like the mirror of the anti-matter of the subtle bodies. One is solid, one is light.

New research in genetics, such as Rupert Sheldrake's theory of morphogenetic fields, points to the reality, traditionally expressed only in spiritual terms, that the pattern or "program of form" appears first of all in the morphogenetic fields (the substance of the subtle bodies), before it becomes dense enough to imprint its message in the DNA of cells.[3] In this way the subtle bodies give life to the physical body. The physical body merely duplicates the program which resides in the etheric and higher bodies. This theory means that the health of the physical body depends entirely upon the health and vitality of the subtle bodies.

As long as the physical body remains heavy and the subtle bodies remain light, each body expresses its right function and we feel balanced and centered. Often, however, unexpressed emotional patterns remain in the astral body as crystallizations of energy, just as negative or obsessional thinking patterns cloud the mental subtle body and unintegrated spiritual inspirations remain "stuck" in the higher subtle bodies.[4] When we begin to accumulate heaviness in the subtle bodies, this heaviness will be duplicated in the physical body, through the crystallization of energy. The first role of the overtone of pure sound is to dissolve this crystallization of energy which can manifest as destructive energy patterns in the physical body.

Sound can diminish the adherence of the negative energy patterns in the aura of the physical body. Later, because the duplication of these negative patterns no longer takes place in the physical, the physical body will be healed.

Western medicine has been slow to recognize the importance of the subtle bodies' role in healing. Doctors may remove a cancerous tumor surgically from the physical body but do nothing to dissolve the crystallizations of energy in the subtle bodies that are the cause of the tumor. Thus the cancer can be re-duplicated again in the physical body - perhaps a few years later, and perhaps in another area of the physical body because energy moves, but nevertheless, the cancer could reappear.

Sound will help to change the negative programs of our lives. This precise work of decrystallization of old patterns in the aura can only be done through acoustic sound made of the natural elements, wood, earth, metal, water or by the sound of the human voice or certain birds and dolphins. (The ultrasounds of dolphins are comparable to certain very high natural overtones and so they carry a strong healing power. The only difference between their sounds and the sounds of natural instruments, humans or birds is that the dolphin sounds are carried through water. This medium makes it difficult for dolphin sounds to have a lasting effect on humans since we no longer live in water).

Energy

The Divine Will, or universal energy, expresses itself through the highest vital forces of chi, love and light. These three rays of light energy are carried to the physical and subtle bodies through several energetic forms including:

Energetic Form	*Body*
sun light	(aura)
year quality	(temperament)
seasonal elements	(element)
day wave	(meridian)
specific hour	(organ)

The different life force energies of very high frequencies are received and transformed through the subtle bodies and chakras into a vibratory level that human density can store and use. Later, when the final transformation takes place, this energy runs through the etheric body to animate the physical body, revitalizing the channels of energy (acupuncture meridians), the nervous system and the blood.

When the transmutation from subtle energy to dense energy is completed, occasional answers to our human questions may arrive naturally as insights through our minds. We all have the ability to receive and understand the divine messages in our minds and hearts. Whether or not we allow ourselves to tune with these life forces will determine the length of delay of perception and understanding of this precious information.

Sometimes information can stay on hold for a long period, even a lifetime, when one is not listening. When we interfere with the process of "divine intervention" through repetitive negative thinking patterns, we stop the positive flow of life and begin to manifest small disturbances or crystallizations in our energy which can develop into physical pathology.

This interference explains how karma manifests itself. The more we resist the natural flow, the heavier the karma will be. By working with chi, love and light we learn to synchronize with the flow of life through non-resistance. In this way healing becomes a dance of chi between the healer and the healed, bringing the forces of the cosmos and our planet into resonance through the human being, where light, chi, love and consciousness are one.

Chapter One

The Healing Synthesis: Sound, Color and Movement

Because of my background as a musician, my early research focused only on the influence of sound on the different levels of the human being. Part of this research took me into the biology laboratory where I took the cell pictures seen in Book I of this series. When I saw how each sound produced a different color and movement or shape in the electromagnetic fields around human cells, I became interested in the link between sound, color and movement.

Later, as I began teaching the practices of pure sound such as Kototama, which are described in Chapter Three, for healing and self-awareness, I understood quickly that the use of sound alone was not enough to affect a deep and lasting transformation on the major levels of our being - physical (cellular), emotional and mental. It became obvious to me that sound, as vibration, works best not as an isolated tool, but as part of a synthesis - or complement - for the vibrational qualities of chi movement and color.

Vibration expressed as sound occupies a specific interval in the continuum of the vibrational spectrum from earth to sky. Imagine a wavelength vibrating vertically from earth to sky. This wave would vibrate as sound, until approximately fifty octaves. Above this point, vibrating at a faster rate, this sound wave would become a color wave. Color speeded up vibrationally would become light. Vibrating at a slower rate than sound is the chi level or energy of human movement. Sound, understood in this context, occupies only a portion of the vibrational continuum that could be developed into tools for healing or fine tuning awareness.

It follows that the use of sound or music alone to promote healing would affect only a certain level of being, but not the "whole" person. I have found that the use of sound alone creates a shorter lived, more ephemeral effect than if I add the tools of other energetic levels such as color and movement. These other tools help to integrate and make more permanent the work with sound.

If we intend to integrate our work with sound into the density of the physical body, it helps to add specific exercises with chi such as Tai Chi, Chi Gong and Tao Yin Fa to "fix" the sound into the matter. If we want to experience the effect of sound at the mental level we need to work together with color to secure the sound influence at this more subtle level.

Even though everything is a part of the whole, I can give an arbitrary model: Chi movement is linked with the physical and etheric body. Sound is linked with the emotional/astral body (even though it can travel very far to higher realms). Color is linked with the mental body. The physical body is the point of integration of the movement. The astral-emotional body is the point of integration of the sound. The mental body is the point of integration of the color.

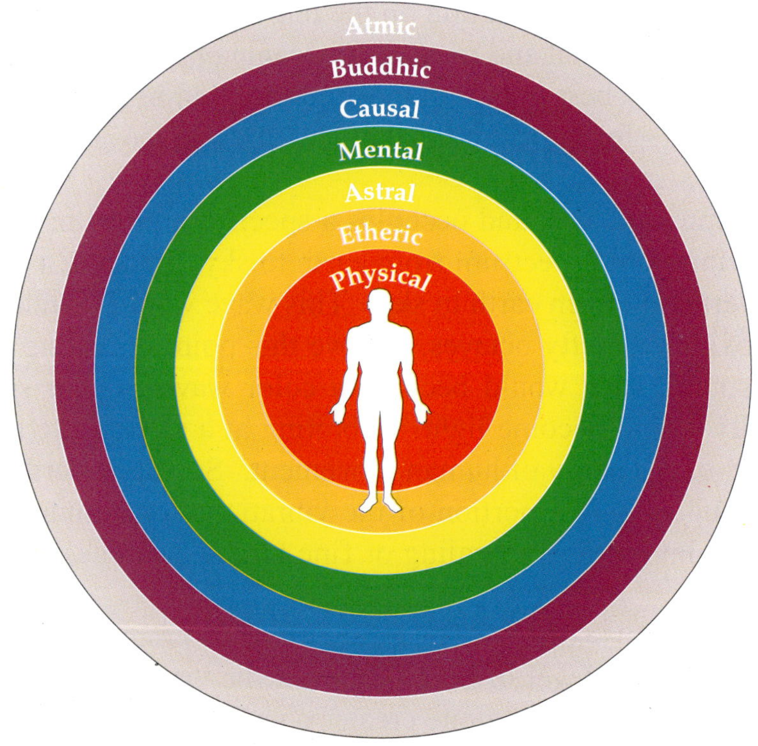

Sound is universally linked with emotion. Different pieces of music affect different emotional responses in people. When we listen to a concert, for example, the emotional response is strong and shifts as the music changes. When we see a color light show or a painting exhibition, our emotional response would be more mental, less dense than for a musical concert. It would elicit lighter emotions such as wonder, awe, or curiosity.

When I say that movement works on the physical and etheric body, I refer essentially to movement based on chi. In the case of the Tao Yin Fa chi movement, each figure is linked with a specific mudra which gives an electric signal to the brain and creates a real connection between the brain and the different systems of the body.[5] This link integrates the purpose of each movement into the cellular and later the molecular level.

Dancing to music does not have the same effect. Dance expresses the personality of the dancer and the energy is expressed more externally. Chi movement works with the inner essence. Here energy is experienced internally. Dance often expresses feeling, emotion and power. Chi exercises work more with the transmutation of these feelings. Dance incorporates muscles and structure. Tai Chi or Tao Yin Fa incorporates the subtle flow of the energy of the meridians and the energy around the body.

Practitioners of chi exercise can use sound to continue the effect of the chi from the physical to the emotional body and even into the mental if they add color. Sound healers can send the sound more deeply into the physical body, into the organs and cells and even the DNA, by directing it with chi movement. Likewise, healers who work with color can use sound to continue the effect of the color from the mental to the emotional body and even to the physical body if they add chi movement.

Scientists have yet to develop techniques sophisticated enough to investigate the inside structure of cells in order to study further what happens as sound is directed through chi into the body. We need a more thorough analysis of the DNA, RNA, protein and amino acids, since they shed light onto what is happening inside of the cells. There are implications that the induction of sound at the cellular level appears to modify information stored in the DNA, a hypothesis which could provide a powerful step toward a lasting healing process.

Scientists in such fields as biophysics and biotechnology are, at the moment, still lacking tools sophisticated or subtle enough to enter more precisely the vibrational world. However, since scientific, rational "discoveries" usually follow intuitive, irrational theories, it is good in the meantime to continue a practice with sound, color and movement to experiment for yourself. In this way we open the energy fields for the future!

Sound, color and movement move and work together in a natural synesthesia. Just as we cannot really separate body, mind and spirit in the healing process, so too the boundaries separating these three vibrational tools are not solid.

There is also a musical rationale which can provide a basis for combining vibrational tools. One sound used alone produces immobility. We are returned to the mirror of ourselves. There is no motion. If we use two sounds, we create an interval and, according to the quality of the interval, movement begins because an interval creates motion.[6] There is a full interaction between two sounds. This same interaction can be created using sound and color. Just as two sounds are more powerful than one in terms of moving energy, so two or three tools, such as sound, color and movement, are more powerful.

The same rationale is true for human relationships. If someone is alone, there tends to be an immobility in his or her consciousness. As soon as another person is present, an interval is created - a moving dynamic begins. When we take into consideration that every person resonates to a specific fundamental sound frequency (a concept which is developed in Book I), the interval created by the meeting of two people could be a deciding factor as to whether their relationship will be harmonious or discordant.

The Mirror of Sound

Another consideration for integrating sound work with color and movement is that of where or to whom you send your sound. If you speak to someone while looking at a gray wall, the sound of your voices or the sound you make with an instrument (or even the vibration of your idea) will be in resonance with this gray wall.

If you speak while facing a rainbow, there are more aspects of the sound which could be received and reflected because you have this different mirror. Perhaps your sound and purpose would be attracted to, or synchronize with, a certain vibration of one of the colors. As you speak or sing, this color will help to fix the effect of the sound into the space around you.

This mirroring relationship means that you must be aware that choices have to be made in the use of sound and color together. The association of the two will create a stronger resonance which will be recorded deeply in the aura. The question about healing with sound and color is not to know whether they produce an effect; they always do. The real question is to know whether the effect is lasting and is integrated by the physiology. An ephemeral effect that only pleases the healer is not valuable.

The same correspondence occurs with movement. If you make a sound while sitting motionless, the effect will be completely different from sounding while doing Tai Chi or Tao Yin Fa. There will be a level where these two arts, movement and sound, meet and at this meeting point the sound will be integrated by the interaction.

The perception and integration of vibration or ideas depends on the mirror of resonance offered by the receiver as well. I teach in several countries to speakers of different languages such as Russian, German, English, French, Swiss German and Norwegian. I observe that the level of perception and integration of work with sound is different with each root language.

Each language integrates a particular aspect of the sound and sends that resonance back to me. Each group, then, teaches me something different and offers another understanding of what I am teaching. This difference probably occurs because sound (or color or movement) touches the vibrational level of each language's roots - roots which create the way of listening, thinking, understanding and even the mythology of each culture.

Using sound is easy. But making sure that its intended message is integrated is another matter. When you are using sound for healing you must take into account who receives the sound and work with the resonance mirrored back if you want to ensure the result you intend. If you do not have the right mirror in front of you, you may lose part of the message you are trying to send. In addition, if you want to integrate your work with sound fully into the body, it makes sense to add movement and color to carry these sound messages into all levels of being.

When the majority of people understand the nature of vibration, this knowledge will open the awareness of civilization to higher possibilities and states of harmony.

Chapter Two

Preparation for the Healing

Inner Preparation for the Healer

When a healer scans the subtle bodies of a patient or takes the Chinese pulses, he or she is in the same state as a composer or musician awaiting inspiration: attentively waiting and listening. This state is like a meditative state of emptiness. When healers can access this inner emptiness, the pulses be taken accurately. When healers are experiencing too much inner activity or disturbance, they will take their own pulses through the patient, especially when they are too intense, too eager to do well. When healers try too hard, they want to give so much that they often give their own energy away and read it in their patients' pulses. This over eagerness is why healers often feel burned out at the end of a day's work.

Healers who are preoccupied with inner complications or problems cannot heal. They cannot find the right diagnosis because they are not empty. Almost all of the great spiritual teachings teach the value of emptiness. For meditating, writing, painting, composing music or taking pulses, emptiness prepares the space for clarity.

Preparing for Healing Treatments

There are several other ways a healer can prepare the space for healing to occur.

1. Clear the room with a gong in the frequency of A 440. Ringing the gong around the room will create a new field, cleared from any astral debris, other unclear energy or disturbing crystallizations of energy in the space. Avoid electronic or electric machine noise such as refrigerators, heaters, etc. because they interfere with the acoustic resonance of instru-

ments and voices. Avoiding these noises also protects the field of the patient during the healing.
By ringing the gong or a bowl in A 440 (moving in spiral around the room), a welcoming energy is created. From the photos in the cell experiments shown in Book I, *The Role of Music in the Twenty-First Century,* we also know that the frequency A 440 emits a pink color often associated with healing and, because it is associated with the frequency of the spin of the electron, will recreate new conditions of life wherever you ring this sound.[7]

2. You, as the healer, can center yourself by linking through your consciousness with Tantien, or hara, the gravitational center of the body. The Tantien or hara is the inner space between the navel on the front of the body and Mingmen on the back.

3. Have the patient use Chinese Breath to purify the organs and clear his or her energy before the treatment. This clearing breath will also help the healer make an accurate diagnosis.

Most of the time people are fatigued, not because of a lack of energy, but because of an excess of unused energy. This energy remains closed inside the body. When the organs are purified with Chinese Breath, this energy is freed. Chinese Breath used together with the first series of Tao Yin Fa is a treatment complete in itself. (Tao Yin Fa is described in Book II).

Chinese Breath

ORGAN	SOUND	PITCH	COLOR	FOCALIZATION POINT
Lungs	See *	G	White	Women, side of both shoulders- 14 of the lungs meridian Men, between nipples 17 of the conception meridian start on the right
Kidney	Schwee	D	Black	Perineum
Liver	Ksu	A	Green	Bladder meridian 11-26
Heart	Ha	C	Red	20 Governor - Paihui Top of head
Spleen	Who	F	Yellow	Solar plexus
Pericardium	Xe	E	Ruby Red	Mingmen - between second and third lumbar vertebra

* The sounds here are not actually sounded, but expressed through the breath.

A slight difference may occur in the sound correspondence depending upon the geographic origin of the Chinese teacher. A teacher from North China will pronounce these sounds differently than will a teacher from South China.

4. Take the three pulses: Hara, throat and feet
Stand on the right of the patient to give him or her space. If you sit on the left side, it is too near to the patient's heart and oppresses the heart energy.

First harmonize with the patient by breathing into your Tantien or hara and then synchronizing with his or her breathing. Slowly put your right hand onto the patient's hara, coming from the etheric down to the physical level. The hara gives the pulse of the earth element. Determine how much energy is in the hara. Then take the throat pulse (Ren Mai 22) - the yin pulse, while still holding the hara pulse with the other hand.

Finally, take the feet pulse (Stomach 41), the yang pulse, while still holding the throat pulse. Determine whether the energy is in the upper or lower body and compare whether there are any imbalances on each of the three pulses. Pre-balance the energy, using your consciousness to move the chi into the right place.

5. Take the acupuncture pulses.[8]

6. Scan the subtle bodies layer by layer with your hand from the etheric level to the highest subtle body that you can reach and notice at each level the areas of crystallization of energy in the fields. Move in the direction from the feet to the head and then from the head to the feet for each level. You will find points of crystallization of energy in the different levels and these points, if connected, create something like a drawing or shape in the fields such as that shown on page 68. This pattern indicates the form of the energy wavelength which is the particular crystallization that is disturbing the patient.

7. Treatment.

After the diagnosis, begin the treatment from the physical to the subtle. When you work on the etheric level (the second part of the healing), it is better not to touch the patient physically again because he or she will be confused and will not be able to synchronize attention or consciousness. When you return to the physical level after beginning in the subtle bodies, the patient could experience side effects and complications.

Also, when you start with sound, generally a patient goes out of his or her physical body and will be jarred if brought back to the physical in a startling way through touch. You risk canceling all of your results.

8. Color Glasses and the sound "SU." To finish the treatment you can reconnect with your hara and the hara of your patient. When a patient is too far away from his or her body you can use the sound SU on the pitch of the season for grounding.[9] It is important for the patient to come back to center when the treatment is finished. If needed you can use also orange color glasses and oranges essences to bring the patient back to the present.

9. Use the monochord tuned with the fundamental key of the season to harmonize body, mind and spirit. The monochord can be placed near the patient unless you have a monochord table. Play softly for three minutes.

10. After the patient leaves, clear the room again with the gong. This should be done even if there is no patient immediately following the clearing treatment.

Chapter Three

Tama-Dõ Healing Techniques [10]

The Tama-Dõ healing techniques are based on the acupuncture structure of Chinese Medicine. The meridian network in acupuncture offers the best foundation possible on which to build and organize the sound, color and movement information. Integrating these three tools into the acupuncture structure gives the most solid base you could wish in this field and makes vibrational healing work easy by virtue of its logical reality.[11]

Technique 1: Tuning Forks on Shu Points

Tuning Forks of different frequencies are applied on acupuncture points called Shu, which are the five element points on each of the 12 meridians. This system is based on a musical system linked with the fundamental note of each meridian.

On each meridian there are five element points: wood, fire, earth, metal and water. Different orders of these elements appear, depending upon whether thr meridian energy is Yin or Yang, as shown in the following charts.

Each meridian contains all of the element points (each meridian, that is, has wood, fire, earth, metal, and water points). Each meridian has a command point, also called the horary point, which is the point of the same element quality as the meridian itself. For example, the liver corresponds to the wood element. The liver meridian is a wood meridian. On this wood meridian, the wood point would be the command point. The heart is fire. On the fire meridian, the command point would be the fire point. Stomach is earth. On the earth meridian, the earth point will be the command point and so on with water and metal. From the command point we will start with the fundamental note of the meridian, building a Cycle of Fifths following the element order on each meridian.

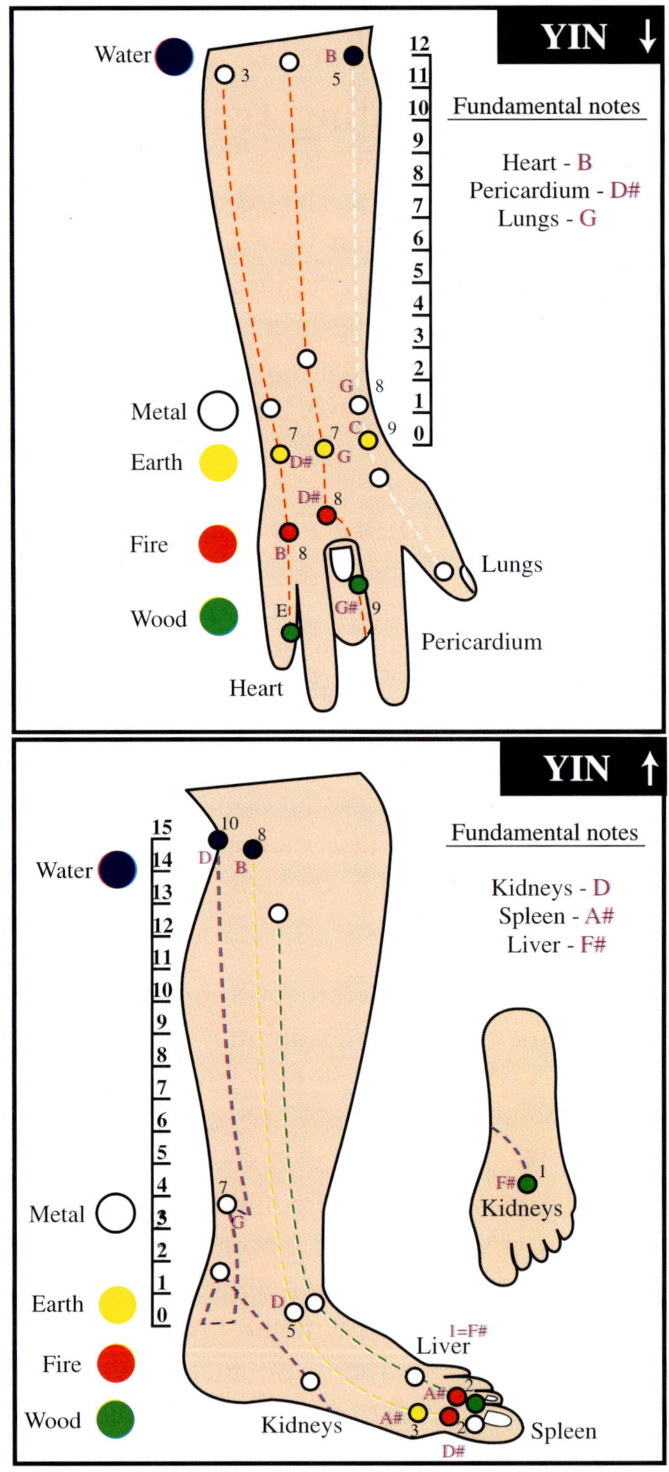

Shu Points and Sound in Yin Meridians

Sound in the Shu Points

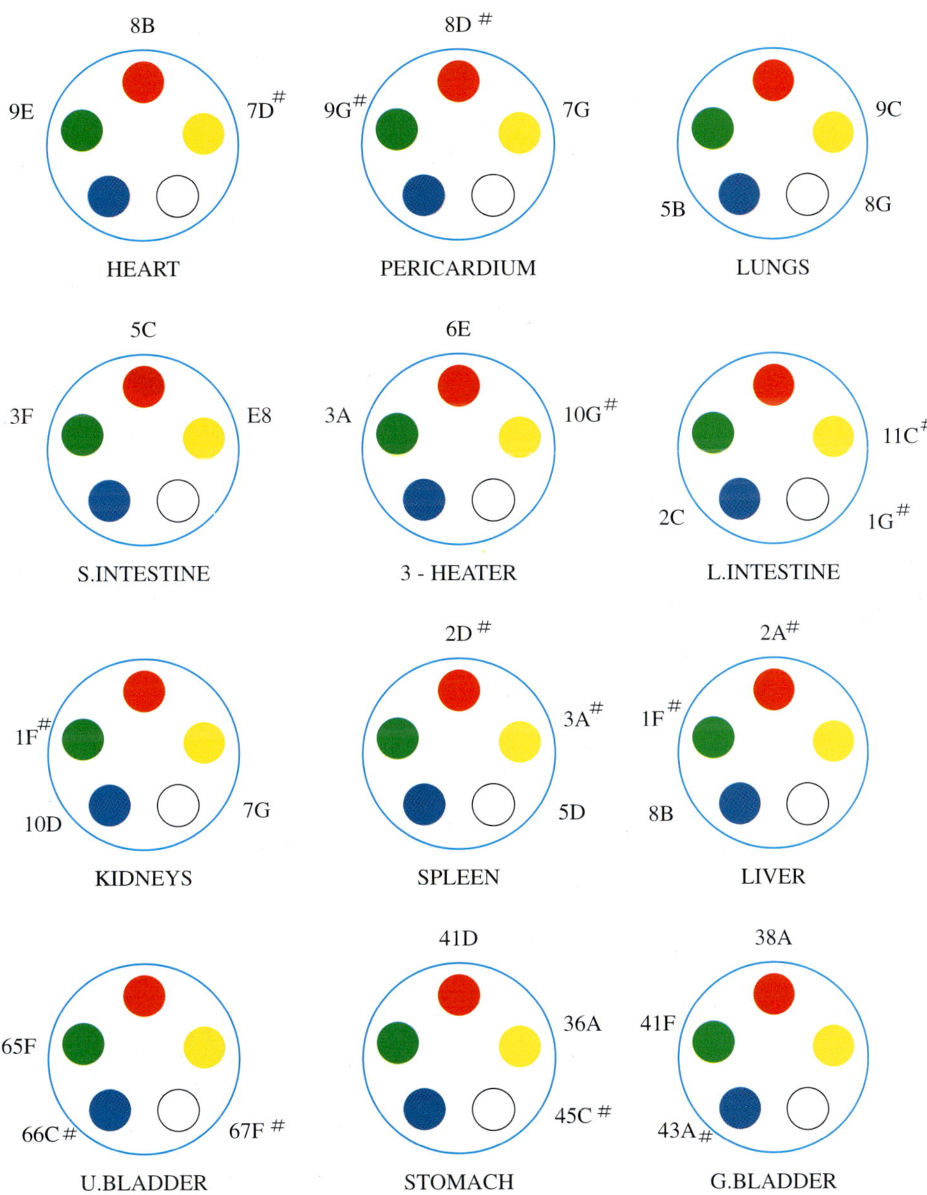

Use the fifth to simulate with the element before the command point
Use the third to sedate with the element after the command point

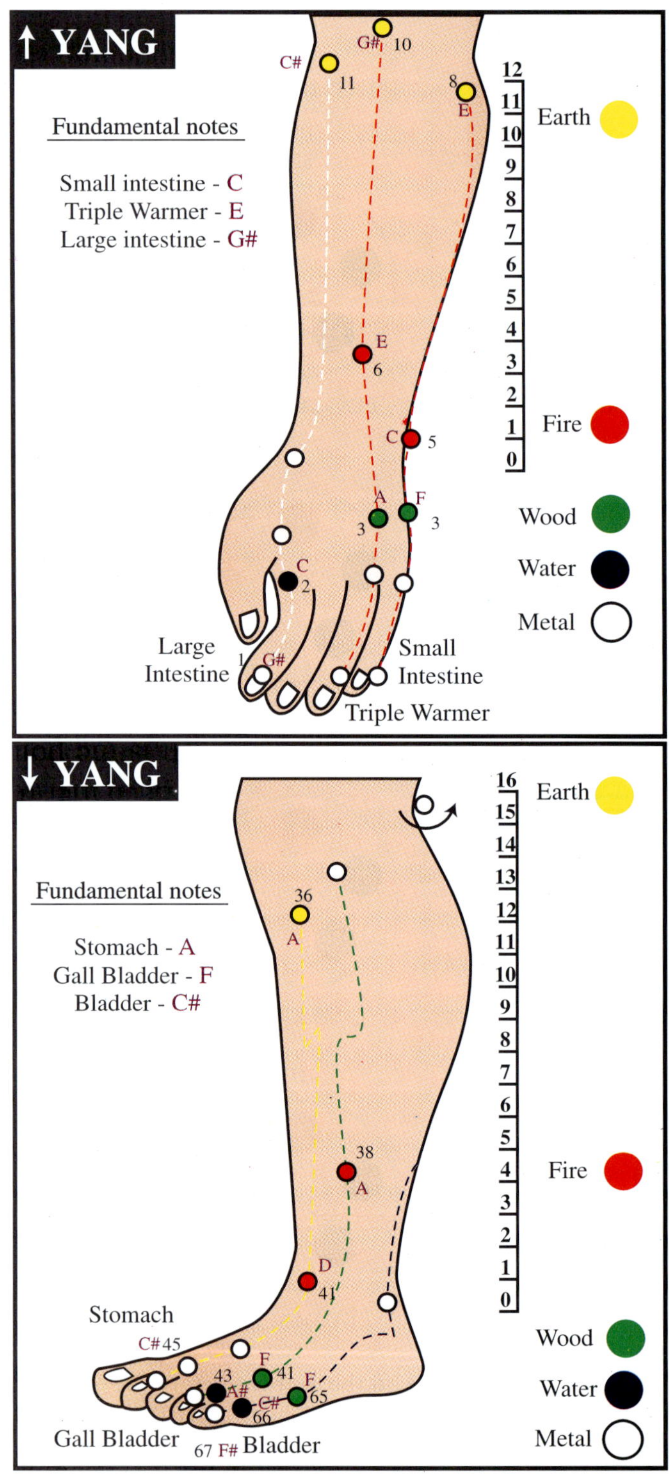

Shu Points and Sound in Yang Meridians

Sound in the Shu Points

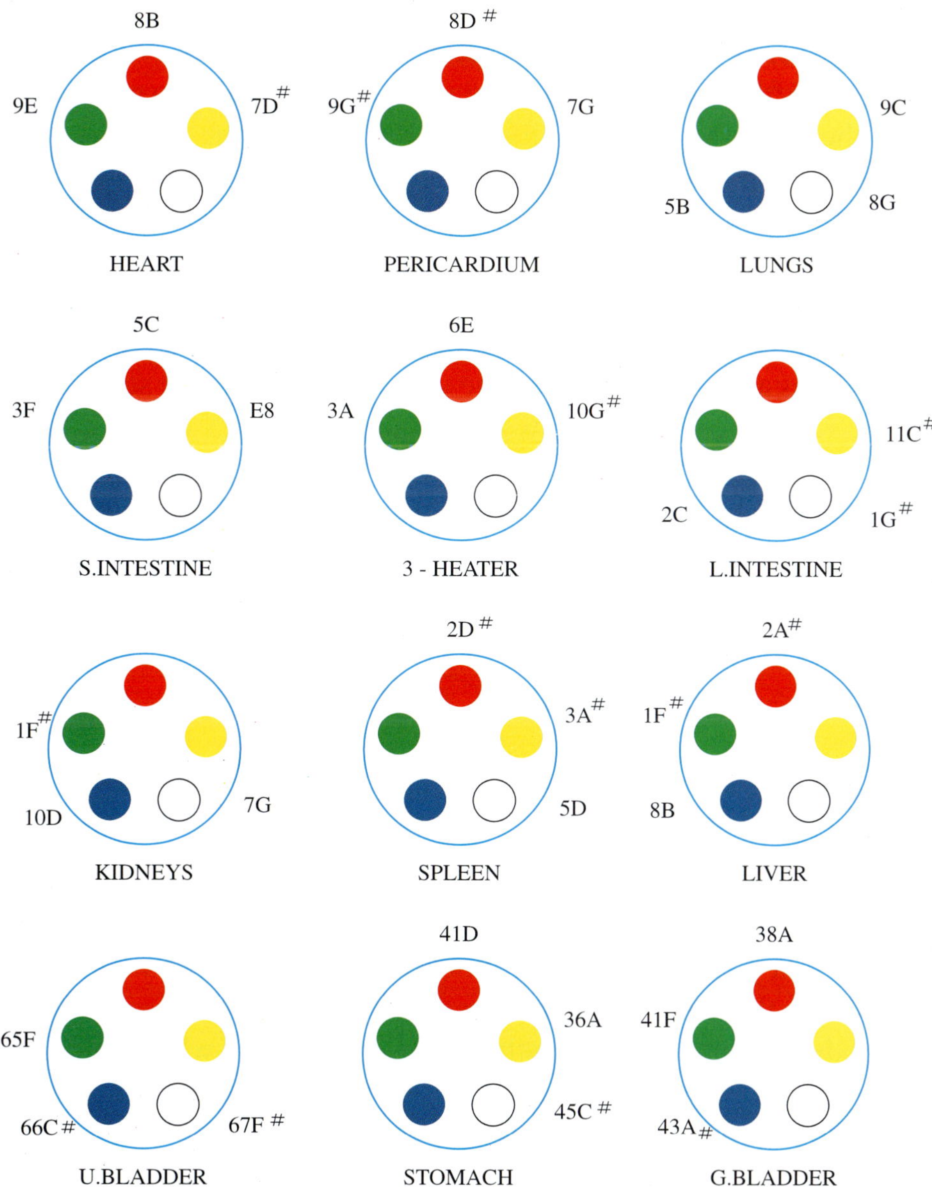

Use the fifth to simulate with the element before the command point
Use the third to sedate with the element after the command point

Tuning Forks and Shu Points

The fundamental note of each meridian is applied on the command point (the horary point) of the meridian. To move energy along the meridian, we need to create a musical interval between two points. We use the interval of the fifth to stimulate and the interval of the third to sedate the energy in the meridian.[12] We will create a fifth with the element before the command point, or a third with the element after the commanc point following the Law of the Five Elements.

For example, if you want to stimulate the wood or the gall bladder, you would take the tuning fork A# on the water point and F on the wood point. This creates a fifth finishing on the wood. If you want to sedate the wood, use the tuning fork F on the wood point again and A on the fire point to create a third finishing on the fire point. This will sedate or stop the energy of the wood. In the stimulating you have nourished, or stimulated the wood with water. In the second example you have sedated the wood by using fire, which burns wood. This could stop the inflammation of the gall bladder.

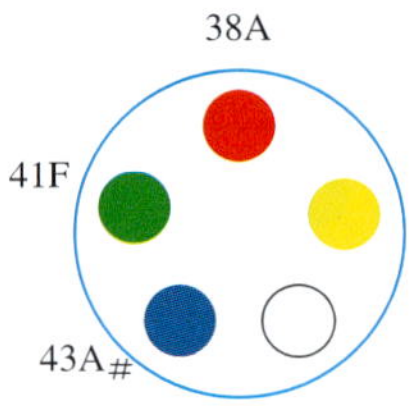

38A

41F

43A#

G.BLADDER

The fundamental note of the meridian is always used on its command point. When you put a tuning fork on the Shu point, it balances the energy because the vibration goes directly into the crystallization of energy. The body regulates the intensity by absorbing only what is needed. The tuning fork works faster than the acupuncture needle because the vibration of sound travels faster than the vibration of the needle.

When you put the tuning fork on the point, the sound also touches the etheric point. This creates a perfect resonance inside and outside of the body. Then the tuning fork vibration can begin to dissolve the crystallization in the etheric as well as in the physical. The tail of the tuning fork conducts the resonance of the musical information into the meridian in the physical body and the fork end sends the resonance into the etheric body and beyond where the real source of imbalance originates.

This resonance will diminish the adherence of the crystallization of energy, which represents negative messages that are duplicated from the etheric to the physical body. Ideally, even in acupuncture, we should attend to the subtle bodies in order to eliminate the real source of most of the energetic trouble.[13]

In this way the meridian system will be able to balance positively the blood and the nervous system. We cannot separate the three systems, blood, nervous and acupuncture, which interact with each other. As you touch one system, you modify the structure and balance of the other two.

Color in the Shu Points

After using the tuning forks on meridians and Shu points, you must use the beneficial color of the element on the command point or along the meridian to fix the effect of the sound.

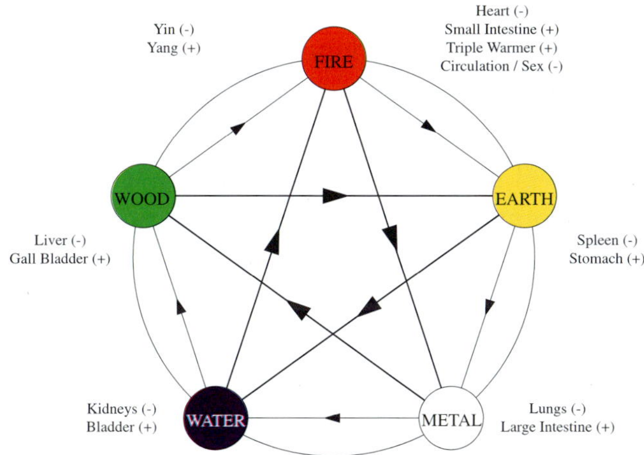

Conclusion

For those who work with energy and learn how to listen, there is a quality of vibration translated into sound which is possible to perceive. When acupuncturists insert needles on the acupoints, sometimes they can hear sound. When they are empty, yet inspired, they can even hear certain precise intervals of sounds along the meridian which have a resonance with the physical structure. Like the meridians, these sounds belong to the inner structure of energy.

Sound can balance energy in exactly the same way as acupuncture needles work by harmonizing the yin and yang If you were aware of the process of synesthesia and could look also at the blue of the sea, the gold of the sun, green grass or the appropriate color for the element you are working with, you would probably ensure an even longer lasting result from the sound with the addition of color. This happens spontaneously if you are enjoying the beauty in nature while singing from your soul a strange or unusual melody. You are unconsciously working to harmonize your own energy with color and sound.

Reprogramming the Cells and the DNA through Sound

Actually what takes place in sound healing is that the sound works in the subtle bodies to repattern the finer levels of consciousness. This repatterning reaches the physical body through the cyclic resonance or "waves" of the overtones of the sound.

We use this cyclic resonance to reprogram the physical body at the cellular and molecular level by applying tuning forks to enter the information on certain specific points. In this way we can reach back through "time" to eight generations of blockages (as implied in the Law of the Eight Elements, or "celestial acupuncture," which is described in Book III, *Sound and Acupuncture.*)

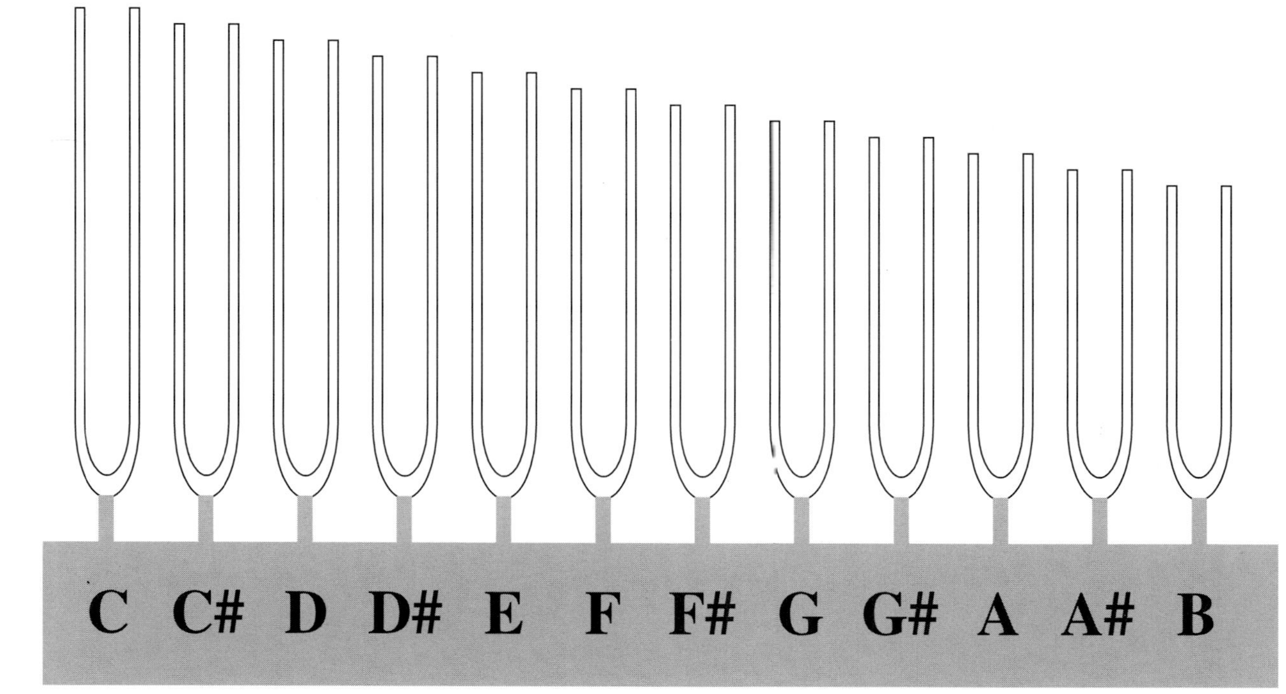

The 12 Tuning Forks Used For The 12 Command Points of The 12 Meridians

Technique 2: Sound and the Spiral of the Ear

Once while walking on the beach in Exmouth, South England, I picked up a perfectly formed spiral shell. When I put it against my ear to "hear the sea.,"[9] I received an insight as to how the ear works. When I held the shell over my ear and turned it slowly around my ear, I heard two different types of musical progressions, first the overtone progression and secondly the Cycle of Fifths. I let this inspiration incubate and finally it formed the basis for a new technique of healing.

The ear is one of the reflex areas used in acupuncture to represent the entire body. The reflex points of the ear can help release pain quickly and are very easy to use.

The curve around the lobe of the ear responds to the Cycle of Fifths. When you follow a straight line from any point on the outer lobe to the center of the spiral of the ear, there is a progression of overtone as you will see in the chart which follows. So you can hear the Cycle of Fifths running along the outer lobe of the ear and the overtone progression going from any point on the outer lobe to the inner parts of the spiral merging in the central point called "Point Zero" by Dr. Nogier of France. This point could also be called the hara of the ear.

If you were to superimpose the "sea-shell" resonating with musical notes onto the ear filled with the reflex points, you would find the exact corresponding note to the part of the body represented by the reflex point. The reflex point would correspond to the note that crosses the straight line running from the outer lobe to the center of the ear.

An interesting observation is that the Point Zero resonates with the frequency A 440. As I have mentioned before, A440 corresponds to the frequency of the spin of electrons and is also the most harmonizing frequency.[14] The cell photos in Book I of this series show that A 440 is the only frequency which consistently produces a healing pink color in the subtle fields around the cells. Knowing this, it is easy to understand the importance of the correspondence between the center of the ear and the frequency A 440. Point Zero is used very often to balance the general energy, just as chi movement from the hara, or the Tantien, can balance energy in the physical body.

Using Tuning Forks on the Ear Points

The magical aspect of sound in the ear, like sound in the acupuncture meridians, is that by the simple act of re-establishing the resonance in the point, we rebalance immediately the energy of the organ or the part of the body that corresponds to the reflex point. What is actually happening is the re-establishment of the free flow of the fluid of the ear through the vibration of the sound thus reconnecting the natural flow of energy all the way back to the source of the imbalance or pain.

When you listen to a sea shell, you hear the perfect resonance of the different arrangements of the sounding lines. If any one of those musical lines were to be interrupted, you would not sense the pleasing spiral of vibration in the shell.

It is the same principle for the ear: When any one point in the ear is not resonating, the entire resonance of the ear is no longer whole. You must re-establish the vibration to return the ear to its natural state, one that sounds like the perfect spiral of vibration of the sea shell. For this re-establishment I use small thin tuning forks for the ear, sounding on the reflex point the corresponding frequency according to each zone of the ear as shown in the following two charts.

Color

After using the sound, you should shine the color given in the Chinese Law of the Five Elements which is beneficial to the organ corresponding to the reflex point in the ear. This complementary use of color will fix the effect of sound in the body.

Main Points of the Ear

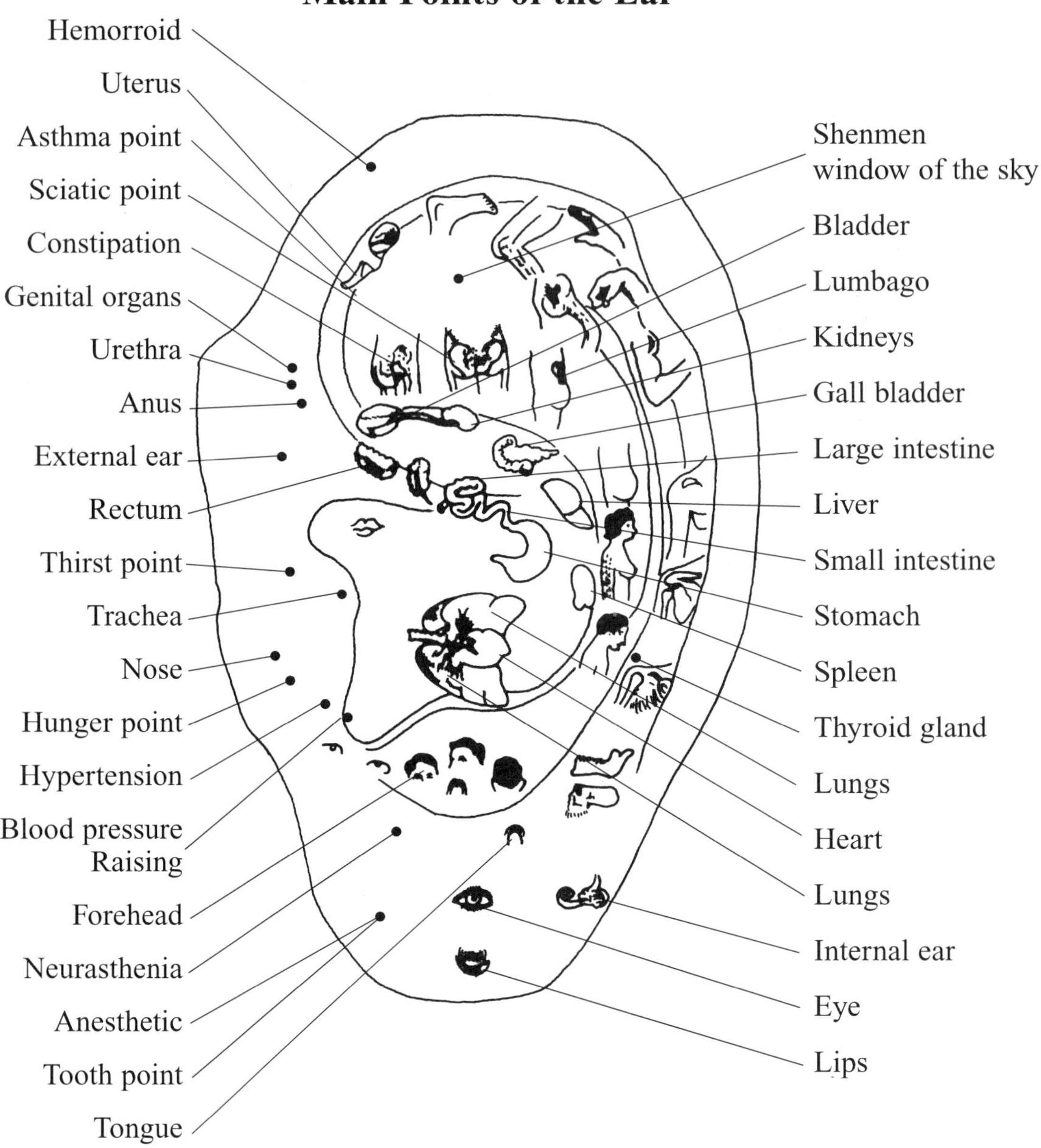

Ring the tuning fork which corresponds to the area of pain as shown in the chart.

Sound and the Spiral of the Ear

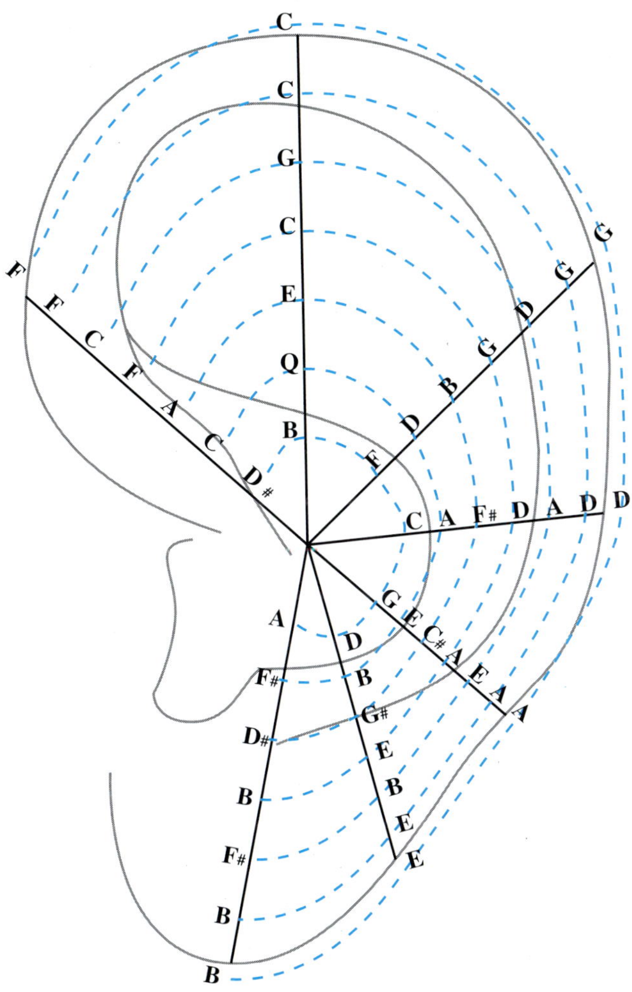

In the ear, the sound reflexology works according to zone and not organ.

Edge of ear:	1	2	3	4	5	6	7	
	F	C	G	D	A	E	B	
	F	C	G	D	A	E	B	
	C	G	D	A	E	B	F#	Overtone progression
	F	C	G	D	A	E	B	
	A	E	B	F#	C#	G#	D#	
	C	G	D	A	E	B	F#	
Middle of ear:	D#	B	F	C	G	D	A	
	Cycle of Fifths →							

Ear, Foot and Hand

I found that a fast way to stop pain is to "circle" it by sounding at the same time the reflex point in the ear and the corresponding reflex point in the foot.[15] When using simultaneously ear and feet reflex points, I use the interval of a third between them to sedate and the fifth interval to stimulate just as in the Shu Points technique.

To sedate, use a third.
To stimulate, use a fifth.

To sedate, use the same quality of reflex point in the ear and in the foot with a third interval between them. For example, the lungs frequency is G in the ear. In the foot, the lungs frequency is B. Play the interval G and B by sounding the G tuning fork before the B tuning fork to have the effect of the third.

To stimulate, using the same example, in the ear reflex point for the lungs you would use the frequency of G and on the foot reflex point for the lungs you would use the tuning fork C. Sound first the tuning fork C and then the G to create the stimulating effect of the fifth.

For foot reflexology, I use big tuning fork with lower frequencies in the scale which corresponds to A 220 or A 110. For the ear reflexology I use fine tuning forks in the scale which corresponds to A 440 or A 880.

WE USE THE SAME FREQUENCIES FOR THE HAND ORGANS, AS WE DO FOR THE ORGANS IN THE FOOT.

Technique 3:
Chakras and Sound

I experimented with several models of sound-chakra correspondences given by different traditions, but was not satisfied with the results. After having used the Cycle of Fifths with such success on the Shu points, ear points and on the musical spine (as shown later), I tried this cycle with the chakras also. I found that this scale of resonance works perfectly to stimulate the chakra energies. The fifth is one of the most important factors of expansion in sacred geometry. The pentagram is the fundamental model for the human being.

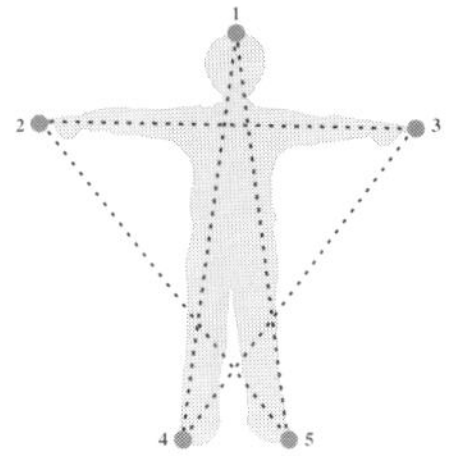

As you will see in the spine chart on page 52, we also use different Pentatonic modes in the tonality of the chakras to sedate or stimulate energies. The Greek modes work more to harmonize the chakras with the endocrine system which is linked with the eight extra meridians in acupuncture. Book I describes in detail the musical modes, Pentatonic, Greek and Hindustani, as well as musical intervals including the Cycle of the Fifths.

Using Sound and Color on the Chakras

We use large tuning forks in the frequency shown on the folowing chart or Japanese, Tibetan or crystal singing bowls (the bowls are more difficult to find in the exact pitch).

Ring the fork or bowl by approaching the chakra only from the back. You will feel if the sound is absorbed or rejected. The same procedure is used with color filters. If the sound or color is needed, it will be absorbed by the chakra. When the chakra has absorbed all that it needs, the sound or color will be rejected. The chakra has a "security system" which enables it to respond to exactly the vibrational input it needs and no more. The time and amount of energy necessary for the chakra to come into balance works by a natural self-regulating process.

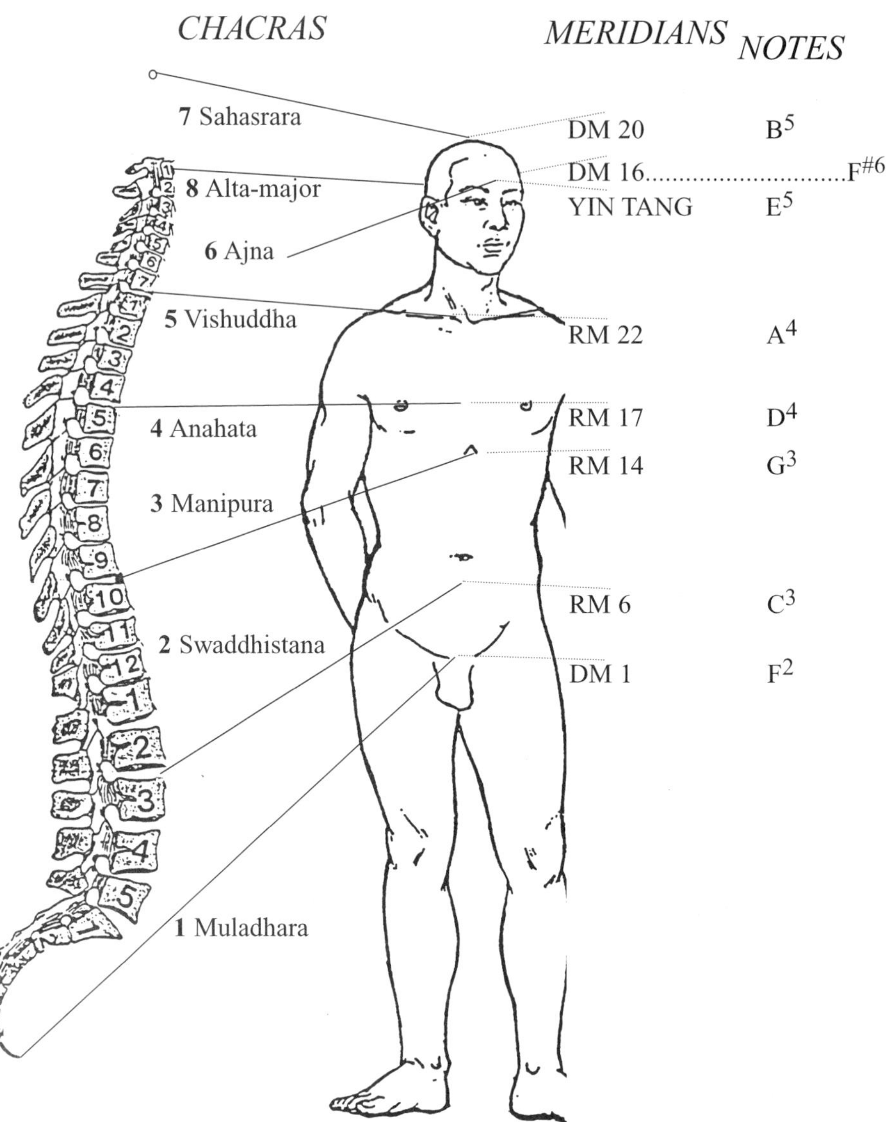

The Chakras and Sound Frequencies

The Cycle of Fifths in the chakra progression is built from the second octave to the sixth octave of the piano in this order: F 87.31, second octave; C 130.81, G 196 third octave; D 293.66. A 440 fourth octave; E 659.26, B 987.77 fifth octave; F# 1479.97 sixth octave.

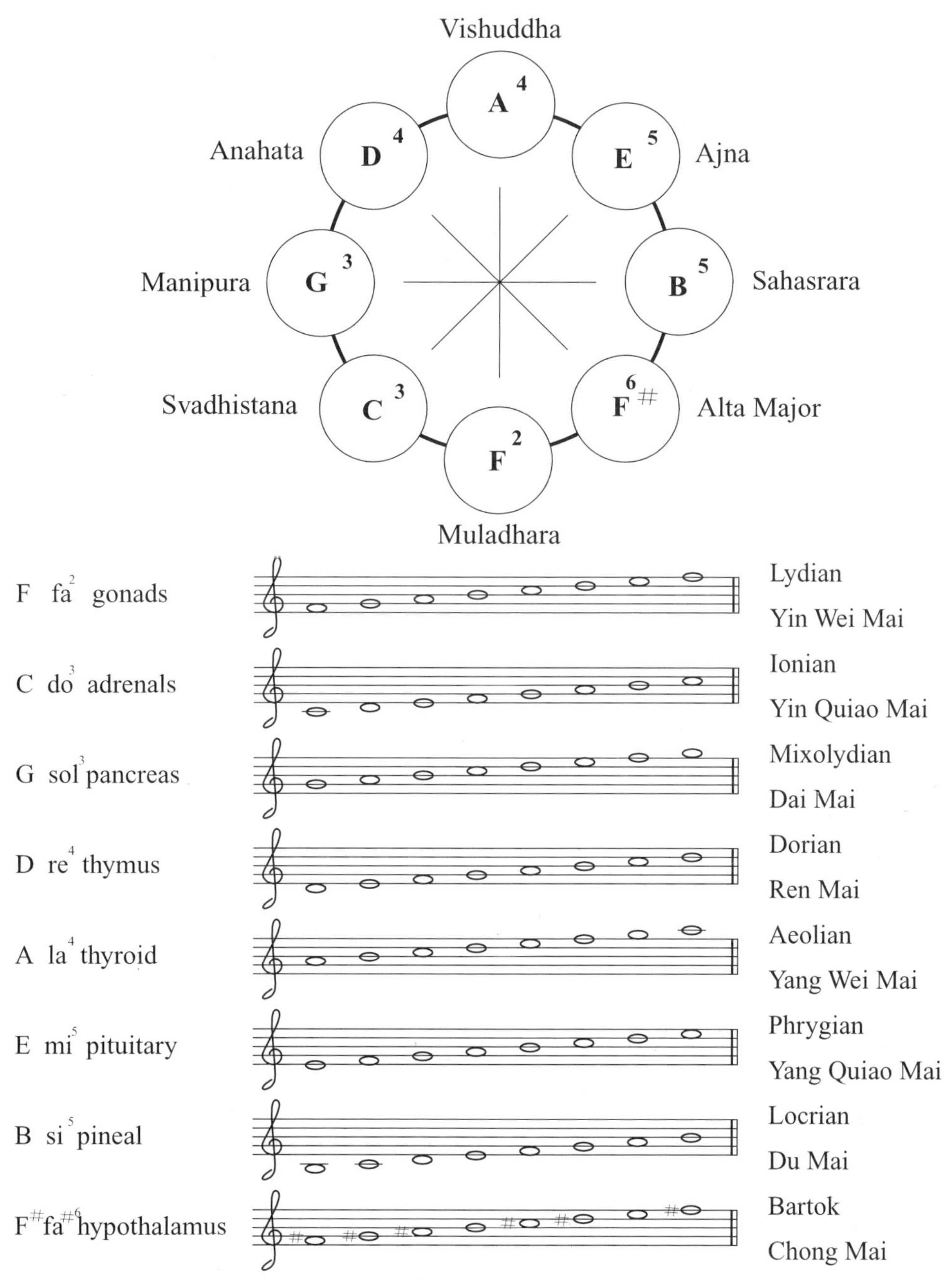

Endocrine Glands - Eight Extra-Meridians
Chakras and the Greek Modes

Technique 4:
T.E.P.

The T.E.P are the Tama-Do Extra Points; the synthesis of healing on three levels, using sound, color and movement together. We use certain key points in the body in precise geometric structure. We use always two sounds, two colors and two points at a time. We are basically working on two major energy flows of the body, the Governor and the Conception Meridians, (Du Mai and Ren Mai), Yang and Yin, and on re-establishing the flow of energy in both to generate a deep healing.

Working on the physical-etheric body with chi, the astral body with sound and the mental body with color creates a whirlpool of energy which will integrate the healing in three different depths, allowing a deep transformation within the session (45 minutes).

I discovered certain key points in the body that relate as precise geometric structure in their strategic function in the body. An acupuncture point is like a musical note with its own vibration and frequency. In music, to sound only one note creates a feeling of immobility. Musical power is activated by the interval between the notes which give stimulation or release. So we need two points to create an interval and to provoke an active resonance.

In our bodies, the same phenomenon happens. The energy lines, the meridians, are like strings of instruments - and the acupuncture points are like the notes on the strings. Therefore, in order to create an active response and resonance in the body, it is necessary to use two points, two sounds and two colors at a time.

Through the utilization of the Tama-Do Extra Points, we allow the two Master Flows of Energy, Ascendant and Descendant, controlled by Du Mai and Ren Mai, to link the etheric and physical and provoke a complete regeneration.

This unique technique of healing on three levels, the T.E.P., is one of the best tools we know to activate the clarity of consciousness on the physical, emotional and mental levels.

TAMA-DO EXTRA POINTS

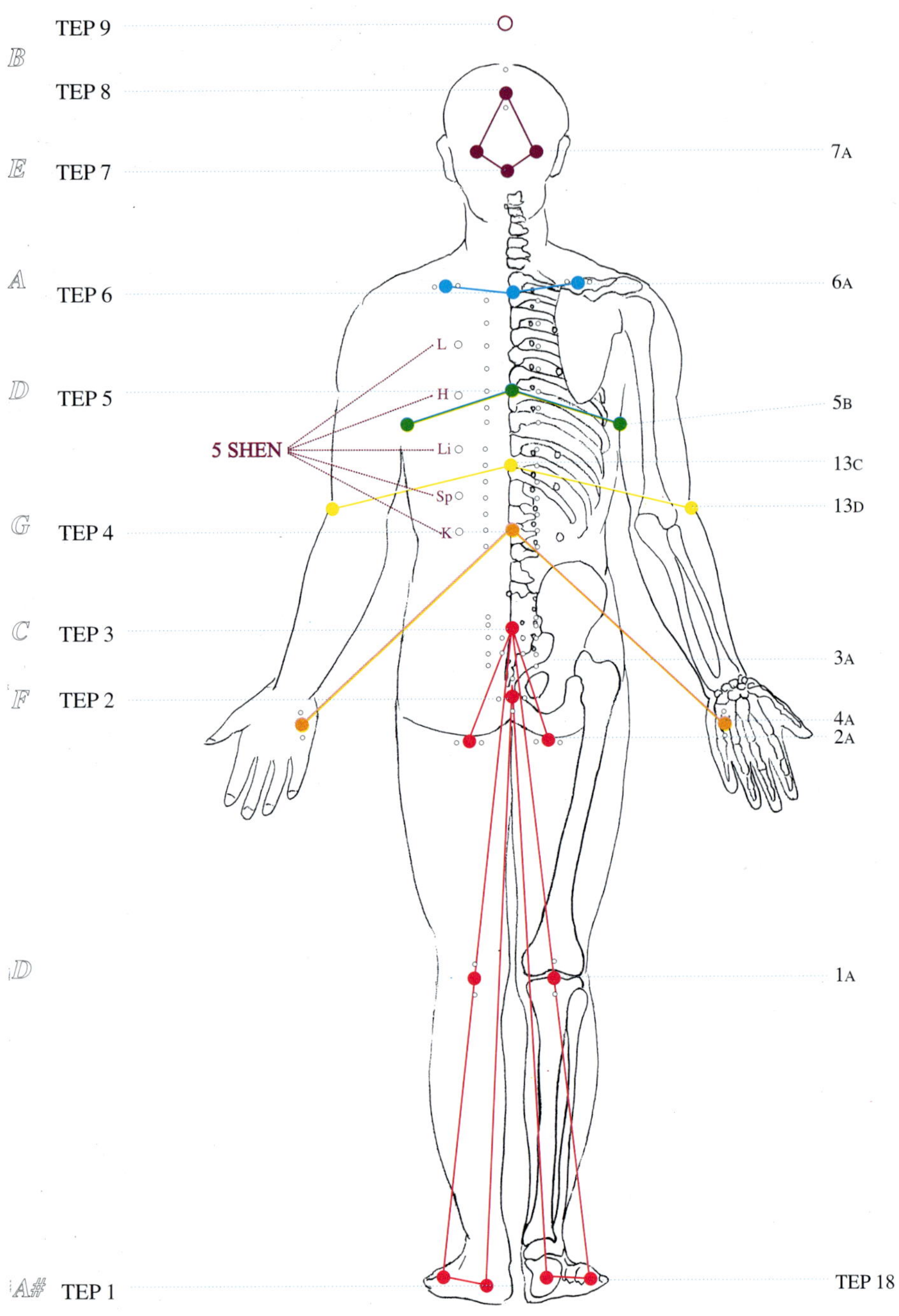

ASCENDING FLOW

TAMA-DO EXTRA POINTS

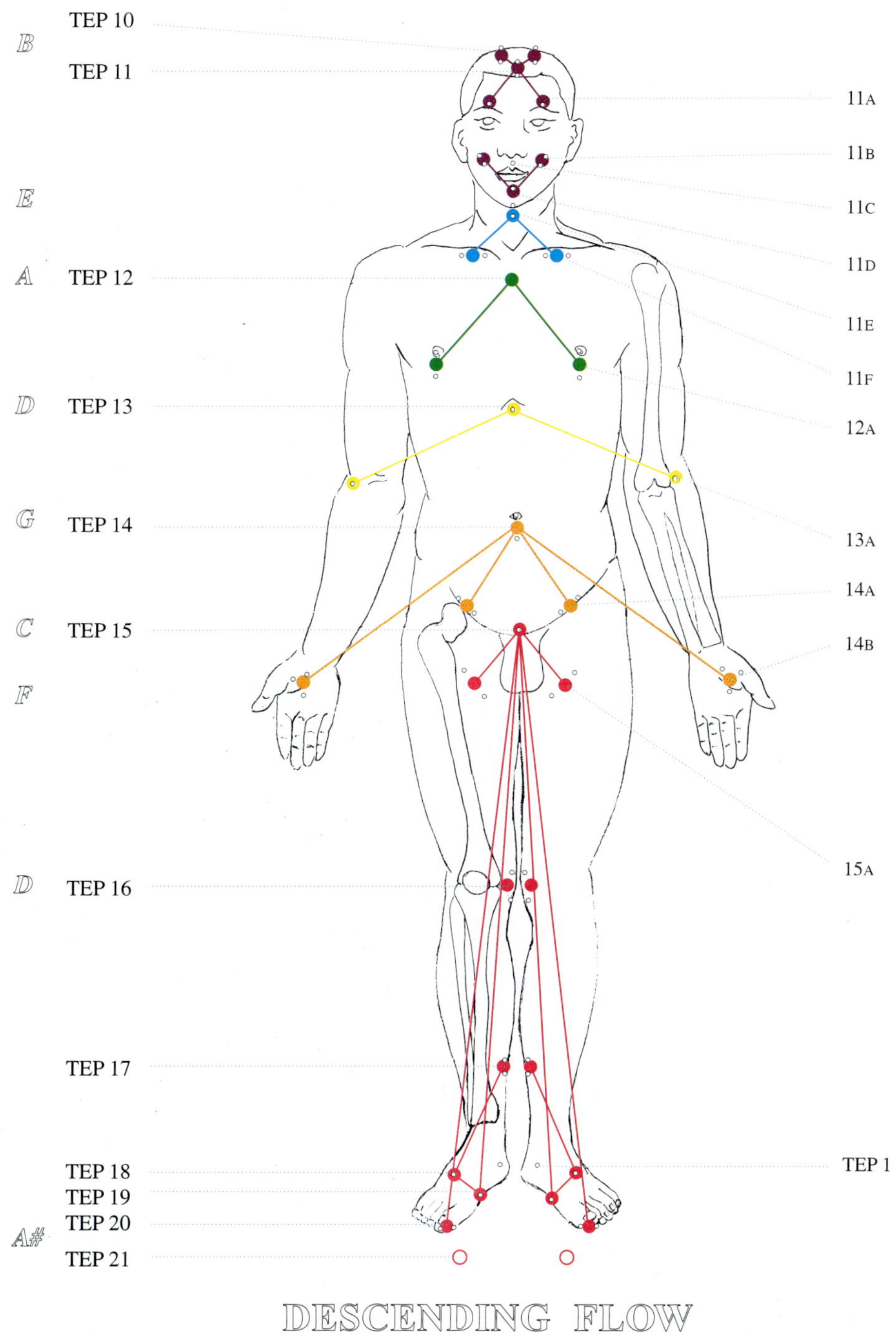

DESCENDING FLOW

As in the Shu Points technique, we use the interval of the fifth, which is the most stimulating interval and will move the energy flow.

The color progresses by zone as shown in the preceding chart, from red to purple.

The sound progresses by zone as shown in the chart in the Cycle of Fifths, from F to B.

The chi is sent by zone to the points as shown in the chart. Move from the feet to the head in the Ascending Flow and from the head to the feet in the Descending Flow, just as you do when using the color and the sound.

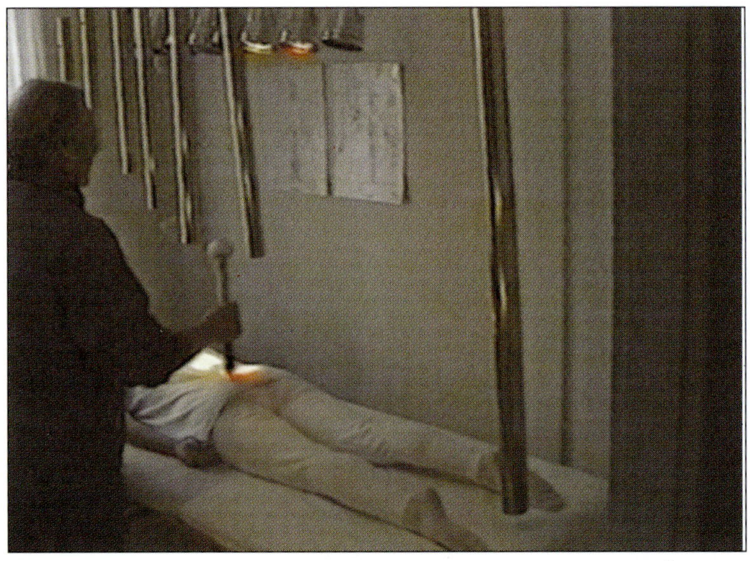

The color flashlight and the sounding tubes in the picture above are used on the master points, the T.E.P., to harmonize the physical with the subtle flows of energy. To complete the TEP we use also the sound table.

The Function of the T.E.P

Ascending Flow

TEP 1 HILL	**B 61 Pushen** **K 5 Shuichuan**	Knee	**B 40 Weizhong** **B 55 Heyhug**
TEP 2 COCCYX	**RM 1 Huiyin** **DU 1 Chanchiang**	Buttocks	**B 36 Chengen** **EP Yankang**
	External Hand	**TW 3 Changzhu** **PE Chingling**	
TEP 3 SACRUM	**DU 3 Yankkuan** **DU 2 Yaoshu**	Sacred Holes	**B 32 Ciliao** **B 33 Zongliao**

TEP 4 BELT DU 4 Mingmen
Ancestral Energy DU 6 Chichung - BL 20 Pishu

TEP 5 BACK **DU 11 Shendao** SEAT OF THE 5 SHEN

Lungs	D 3	D 4	B 37	PoHu
Heart	D 5	D 6	B 39	Shentang
Liver	D 9	D 10	B 42	Rounmenn
Spleen	D 11	D 12	B 44	Yitche
Kidneys	L 2	L 3	B 47	Tchetche

TEP 6 CERVICAL DU 14 Tachui

Wing Roots: **PE Raichingfeng** / **PE Chienchungshu**

DU 16 Fengfu

TEP 7 Alta Major Inspiration Point B 9 Yuchnen

DU 15 Yamen

DU 20 Paihui

TEP 8 Head

DU 19 Houting

TEP 9 Etheric Crown Point Above the Head - The "Door of the Sky"

When there are two acupuncture points given, the TEP point is located between the two points.

Descending Flow

TEP	Area	Main points	Sub-area	Points
TEP 10	Hypophysis	**B 6 Chungguang** **B 5 Wuchu**		
TEP 11	Forehead	**DU 24 Shenting** **B 3 Mechung**		
			Eyebrow	PE 3 Yuyan
			Nose	DU 26 Renzong
			Cheeks	SI 18 Chuanliao ST 3 Chuliao
			Chin	RM 24 Chenquiang PE TiHo
			Throat	RM 23 Lienchuan
TEP 12	Thymus	**RM 21 Huanchi**		
			Clavicle	K 27 Shufu ST 13 Chifu
			Breast	ST 17 Juchung ST 18 Juken
TEP 13	Solar Plexus	**RM 14 Chucheh**		
			Ribs	SP 21 Dabao
			Forearm	LI 11 Shuchih LU 5 Chitse
TEP 14	Navel - Hara	**RM 8 Shejue** **RM 6 Qihai**	Groin	PE Weipao PE Shuhsi
TEP 15	Pubis	**RM 2 Qugu**		
			Inside Thigh	PE Chaioling ST 31 Pikuan
TEP 16	Knee	**PE Liaoliao** **K 10 Yinku**		
TEP 17	Calf	**SP 6 San Yin Chiao** **PE Chiu Wai Fan**		
TEP 18	External Foot	**GB 41 Tsulinchi**		
TEP 19	Internal Foot	**SP 4 Kungsun**		
TEP 20	Big Toe	**PE Mushihli-Hengwen** **SP 1 Yinpai**		
TEP 21	Etheric Point	**Under the Foot**		Door of Earth

Energetic Qualities of the T.E.P.

TEP 1	HILL	Source of water - protected by the "luminous sea"
TEP 1A	KNEE	Between complaint and yang harmony - link with past memory
TEP 2	COCCYX	Unify Yin and increase power
TEP 2A	BUTTOCKS	Adding and sharing by reclaiming the yang of the brain
TEP 3	SACRED HOLES	Inner resonance and regeneration Roots of the inner smile
TEP 4	BELT MINGMEN	Door of Destiny - Linking with Ancestral Energy
TEP 4A	HAND	Central island - Brings back balance and peace even when one doesn't know it
TEP 13C	CHICHUNG	Center of the back - silence of the "Hanging Axis" - Master of the energy of the kidney - Feeling of abundance
TEP 13D	FOREARM	Internalizing energy
TEP 5	BACK SHENDAO	Shen's Voice - Protects Heart - Feeling the freedom of life
TEP 5B	RIBS	Enveloping the expression
TEP 6	CERVICALS	Door of the Big Way - Brings Great Silence Quiets fever
TEP 6A	WINGS	Sacred Command Point of the "Wings"

TEP 7	ALTAMAJOR	Between Silence and the Palace of the Fong - Resting point of creativity
TEP 7A	YUCHEN	Receiving inspiration
TEP 8	HEAD (TOP)	Mind opening on "the 100 Meeting"- Mirror of the physical and spiritual energies - Deep happiness and sense of well being - Complete alignment on one's central axis
TEP 9	ETHERIC CROWN	Door of the Sky - Guidance - Opening at the highest level
TEP 10	HYPOPHYSIS	Receiving back the Divine Light which then travels into the body
TEP 11	FOREHEAD	Superior star which calls one to the center of the Higher Self
TEP 11A	EYEBROW	Perfect integration
TEP 11B	NOSE	Preparing one's vision and energy
TEP 11C	CHEEKS	Receiving the sky
TEP 11D	CHIN	Transforming the nectar - Preparing the energy of the nectar
TEP 11E	THROAT	Communication center - Memory of dreams Assimilation of the nectar
TEP 11F	CLAVICLE	Door of energy - Emotional release
TEP 12	THYMUS	Celestial Sphere - Recharging the battery of immunity

TEP 12A	BREATH	Control and integration (transmutation) of emotions
TEP 13	SOLAR PLEXUS	Fire Point - Expansion of freedom - Energy for merging with the world
TEP 13A	FOREARM	Contains the expression of action
TEP 14	UMBILIC HARA	Sea of energy - Point of emergence of all true manifestation
TEP 14A	GROIN	Containing the will of manifestation
TEP 14B	HAND	Opening the way of the Light toward the Earth Sense of offering oneself
TEP 15	PUBIS	Feeling one's personal power - Giving a direction to one's creativity
TEP 15A	THIGH	Pacifying the descending energy flow
TEP 16	KNEE	Yin Valley - Brings back to earth the Spiritual Memory, helps to concretize and use these memories
TEP 17	CALF	Crossing point of the three Yin - Quieting the mental overflow
TEP 18	FOOT (EXTERNAL)	Concerns tears - eyes- master of wood
TEP 19	FOOT (INTERNAL)	Concerns the beginning and end of things
TEP 20	TOES (BIG)	Stops the flow of thinking - Reveals that which is hidden - Link with the mind - Mystery
TEP 21	ETHERIC POINT OF THE FEET	Opens the water-fluid to link with earth

Technique 5:
Musical Spine

The spine is the central axis of the physical body. The spine is linked with the chakras and the endocrine glands, with the network of the nervous system and with two important acupuncture meridians, the bladder meridian and the yang energy of Du Mai, which is the Governor meridian in the center of the spine.

One of the channels of the bladder meridian actually traces the outline of the vertebrae of the spine from the first vertebra to the sacrum. The points along the bladder meridian on both sides of the spine are known as the energetical reflex points of all the organs of the body. The spine is also the link between the ganglia inside and the chakras outside of the body. Thus, the spine appears to be the link between the inner and outer energy.

The essence of the spine is like solid sound and responds beautifully to sound healing. I use different fundamental notes for each part of the spine. Also, each zone of the spine corresponds with a musical mode and the different notes of this musical mode are applicable to each vertebra.

Some modes will relax the spine, while other modes will stimulate the spine. When playing the modes we can use tubes, xylophone, piano or even tuning forks. Sound and color are used here in a different scale of reference linked with the astral level and no longer with the physical/etheric level like the sound used in acupuncture which is given in Chinese Five Element Theory.

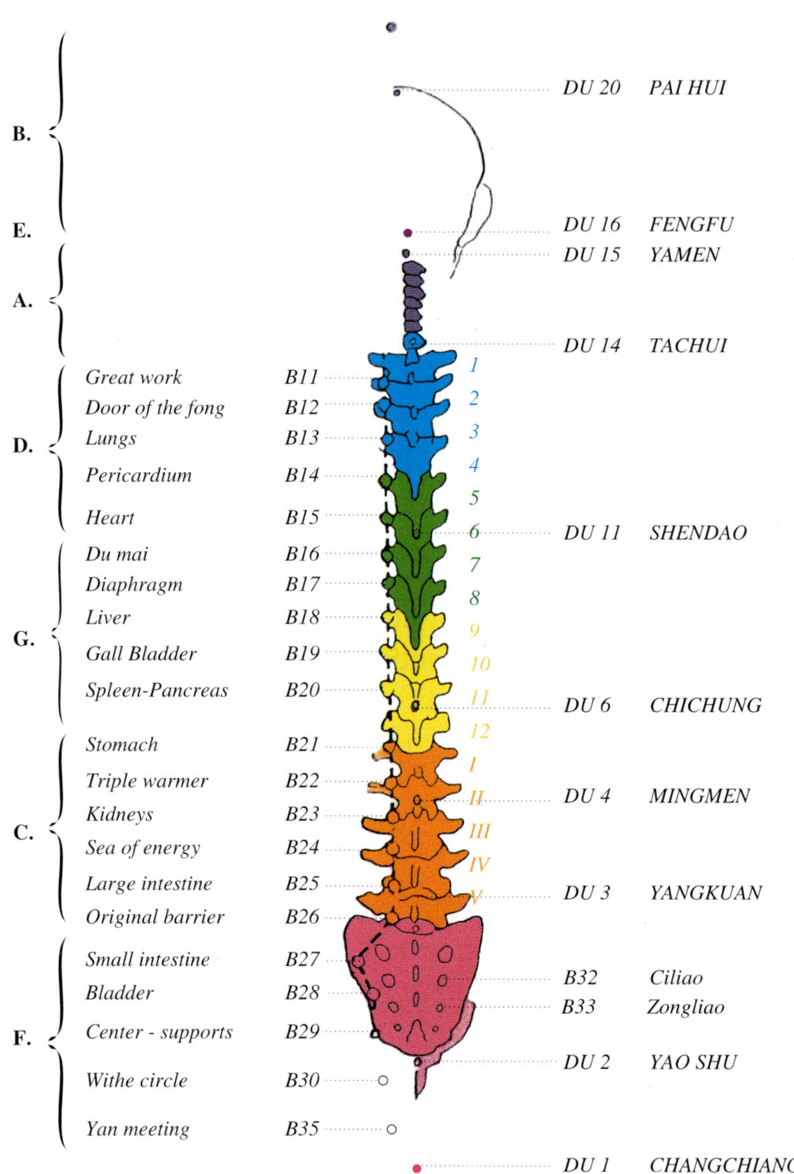

THE MASTER POINTS OF THE SPINE

The zones of the spine correspond and vibrate differently with each season during the year. Each zone resonates with a musical mode, key and color as seen in the following chart. [16]

The sacrum resonates with earth and Indian summer, the color red, and modes Vibhasa and Jog in the key of F.

The orange zone, the five lumbar, resonates with water and winter, and modes Hindol and Gunkali in the key of C.

The yellow zone, thoracic vertebrae 12 - 9 resonates with wood and spring, and modes Bhupala and Durga in the key of G.

The green zone, thoracic vertebrae 8 - 5, resonates with fire and summer, and modes Megha and Bhupali in the key of D.

The blue zone, thoracic vertebrae 4 - 1 resonates with metal and autumn, and modes Sri and Malkaus in the key of A.

The purple zone, cervical vertebrae 7 - 1 plus the head, resonates with the overtone progression from E to B, Sky resonance.

The spine is the witness of karma as well as a strong mirror of ones present life. The spine offers an understanding of physical, emotional and mental problems if you are aware of the zone which is affected. There are two important points linked with the energy of karma in the spine: Mingmen, called the "door of destiny" located between the second and third lumbar and Yangkuan on the fifth lumbar, called the "original barrier." All other points from the base of the spine to the top will develop the ability to unfold this energy of karma during each person's lifetime according with the degree of opening of Mingmen and Yangkuan. We should always send chi to these two points to open the way!

The musical progression along the spine is a gentle yet powerful tool for releasing physical tension in the spine and harmonizing the back area with the most important reflex zone in the human body. The sounds of the musical modes help to awaken memories from past, present and future lives.

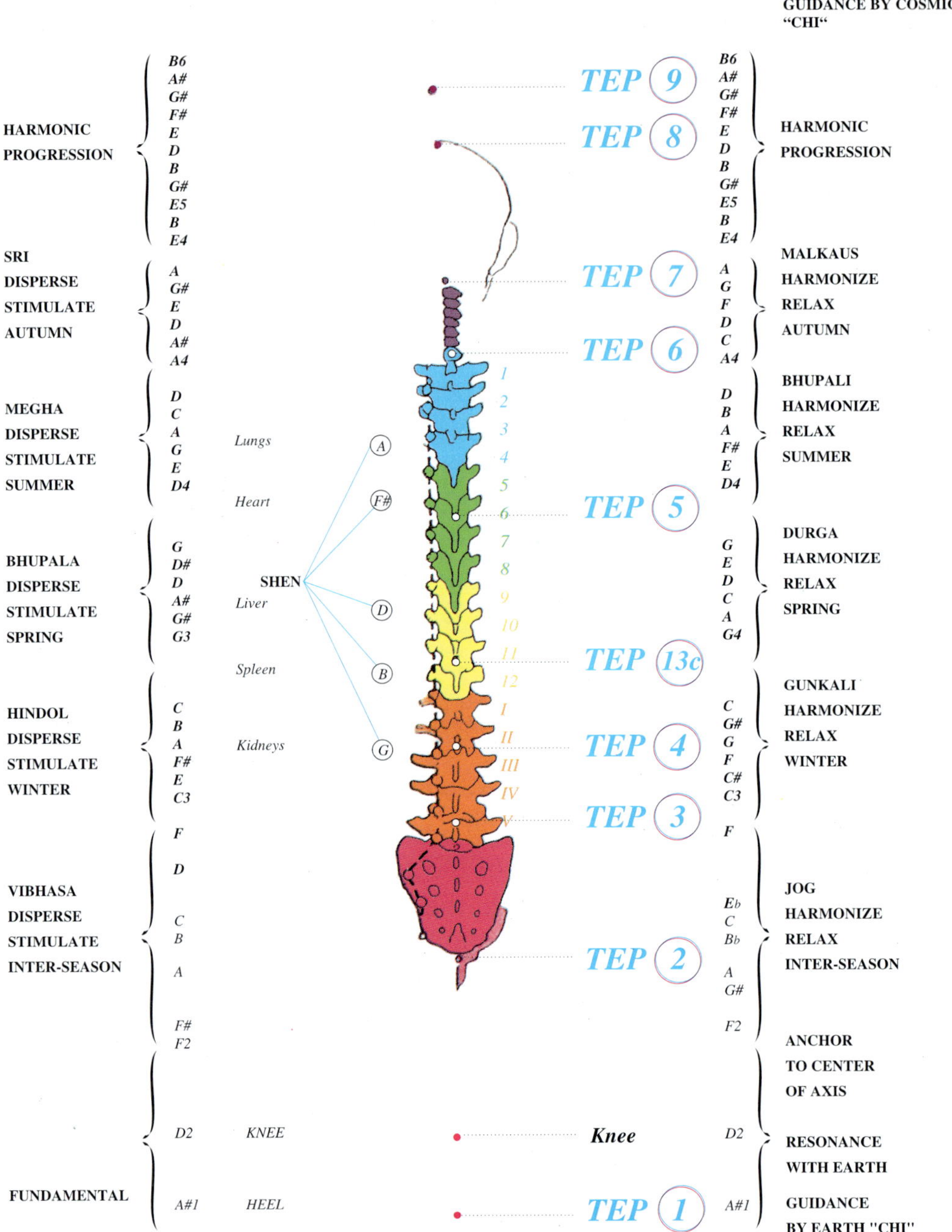

THE SPINE VIBRATES DIFFERENTLY WITH EACH SEASON
EACH SEASON RESONATES WITH A MUSICAL MODE
THROUGH THE CHOICE OF MODE, WE CAN EITHER HARMONIZE OR STIMULATE

THE MUSICAL SPINE

In sound healing there are different scales of correspondence depending upon whether one is working on the physical level, astral level or mental level. The key of each season given by the Chinese works on the physical level according with the Law of the Five Elements. The first spine chart, *The Master Points of the Spine*, shows how to work on the spine from the astral level with sounding tubes. The scale outside of the physical body in the astral level, from the sacrum to the cervical, follows the Cycle of Fifths progression.

In the second spine chart the musical modes are shown in two columns, one to the left of the spine and one to the right of the spine. On the left are all of the modes used to stimulate the different zones. On the right are all of the releasing and harmonizing modes. You will play for each zone the appropriate mode either with the sounding tubes, with the piano or with a monochord table about 30 centimeters from the spine. You can also play all of the modes from the sacrum to the cervical, one by one very slowly in the appropriate rhythm to harmonize or stimulate the spine.[17]

Stimulating Modes

Vibhasa: Key of F
Hindol: Key of C
Bhupala: Key of G
Megha: Key of D
Sri: Key of A
Harmonic progression from E to B

Relaxing Modes

Jog: Key of F
Gunkali: Key of C
Durga: Key of G
Bhupali: Key of D
Malkaus: Key of A
Harmonic progression from E to B

Technique 6:
Healing with Chi Movement

Chi movement is a fast and easy technique for self healing. Tai Chi, Chi Gong and Tao Yin Fa are used to get into contact with the balance of the physical and etheric bodies, the inner self, nature and the cosmos. Chi movements demand that you are present, aware and conscious at all levels. Progress depends only upon your own perseverance in daily practice. Here you are completely active yourself and do not need another person to act as healer.

Chi movement is a master tool for evolution and self healing. Healing chi movements can be found in certain forms such as Zhineng Chi Gong and Tao Yin Fa which are described in Book II. In these types of practices you are in touch with your own chi and cosmic chi. These practices are ancient yet new methods of communication and relationship. When you work with chi, it is good to be aware of the power chi has on the subtle bodies and their breathing process as well as the resonance that chi provokes between the subtle bodies and physical bodies.

One of the main processes that takes place when working with chi is that the astral body receives information and sends it to the brain. The brain then gives back information to the etheric body and from this link we build new energy. A great benefit of this process is the cessation of thinking. The secret is that the repetition of the same movement in slow motion stops the agitation of the mental will after about fifteen seconds and inhibits thinking, allowing the transfer of information between the subtle body and the brain and the brain and the physical body.

Tao Yin Fa, for example, helps to tonify the organs, sedate "negative" energy, stimulate the etheric body and regenerate the physical body. The third series of Tao Yin Fa also works with the star energy of the eight directions. Tao Yin Fa is described in detail in the second book of this series.

Chi movement is linked with the five elements in nature. It is a therapy, complete in itself, closing the circle of the Tao, Yin and Yang, the balance of the universe. We come from the silence and we return to the silence by the universal link with the light through movement. When we move in this meditative way, it is as if we do acupuncture in space.

We revitalize the link to the cosmos through our meridians and come once again into resonance with earth and sky. In the end, true healing is not about what changes only in the moment but what is changed for the future.

Technique 7:
Healing with Voice

Kototama Sound and Acupuncture

Kototama, the Science of Pure Sound, was first introduced to the west in Paris by Sensei Nakazono in 1972. Kototama uses specific sounds to structure the creation of the universe as well as the different epochs of human civilization. Book III describes more completely this esoteric science as it was taught to me by Sensei Nakazono.

The sound structure of consciousness which Kototama describes can be integrated into the Chinese Five Element Theory to create a strong lens through which to view the human being in resonance with nature. Kototama sound can bring information to the body through the five elements. Kototama sound can also be used to stimulate the physical organs and acupuncture meridians.

The Kototama vowel sounds are used to stimulate the Yin organs. A consonant with the vowel stimulates the Yang organs. As you sing the sound from the following chart, visualize the corresponding color and place your hands over the area where the organ is located in the body. You may feel your hands being moved gently into the auric space of the organ. If so, sound more quietly or move into overtoning until you end with your hands far into the aura of the organ, just thinking the sound.

Element	Organ	Note	Color	Sound
Metal	Lungs	G	White	U
	Large Intestine	G#		WU
Earth	Stomach	A	Yellow	WI (we)
	Spleen-Pancreas	A#		I
First Fire	Heart	B	Red	E (a)
	Small Intestine	C		WE
Water	Bladder	C#	Dark blue	WO
	Kidney	D		O
Second Fire	Pericardium	D#	Crimson	HI (HE)
	Triple Warmer	E		HWI
Wood	Gall Bladder	F	Green	WA
	Liver	F#		A

The visualization of the color added to the resonance of your own voice singing these sounds will complete the stimulation of your internal energy system. When you want to sedate or calm internal energy, use the Chinese Breath (page 17).

Sound Structures: Space and Time

Kototama practices could be called meditations of sound which contain cosmic memories of the sound structure of the world as well as vibrational influences of civilizations past, present and future. At the same time, this sound science reaches the deep level of the internal organs of the physical body through a resonance with the five elements and acupuncture.

In an attempt to provide a philosophical overview of the creation of the world using the semantics of sound, Kototama works with the energetic meaning of the vowels and consonants. These linguistic sound units form the roots of all language and also provide a sound structure for understanding creative manifestation of the universe.

Vowels carry magnetic power and thus create the spatial dimension of sound as it continues to spiral through space - beginning with the original sound (the Big Bang, The Word, or Logos). With their electric power, the pure consonant sounds introduce the more human concept of time. So, while vowels open space, consonants mark time.

Esoteric Healing

The practice of Kototama vowel and consonant orders can help to awaken us to our inherent multi-dimensionality. When the pure sounds of Kototama can be linked with our physical structure through the internal organs, this multi-dimensionality can be integrated into the body. It is through the principles of acupuncture and the Law of the Five Elements that the Kototama sounds find resonance with the physical body.

Practicing the sound orders in Kototama involves work with the epochs of human civilization, past and future, called the Moon Time, Sugaso, and the Sun Time, Futonolito. When you work with the sounds of the Moon and Sun Times, you balance your inside energy and produce from this balance exactly what you need for your present. The Moon and Sun orders correspond also to the Alpha and Theta brainwaves.

There is a certain order of vowels and consonants which reflect the Moon civilization of the past and the Sun civilization of the future. The Moon Order consonants are practiced with the vowels of that order to create a powerful electromagnetic activation of resonance with the memories of that past time, which was the epoch when such knowledge as Yoga, Acupuncture, Tai Chi, the Tao, the Kaballa and much of the Shamanic wisdom was discovered. The same procedure is used with the Sun Time vowel and consonant order to create a resonance with the civilization of the future.

Sound Practice I

MOON ORDER

A	TA	YA	KA	MA	SA	LA	HA	NA
O	TO	YO	KO	MO	SO	LO	HO	NO
U	TSU	YU	KU	MU	SU	LU	HU	NU
E	TE	YE	KE	ME	SE	LE	HE	NE
I	TCHI	YI	KI	MI	SI	LI	HI	NI

SUN ORDER

A	TA	LA	KA	NA	MA	YA	HA	SA
I	TCHI	LI	KI	NI	MI	YI	HI	SI
E	TE	LE	KE	NE	ME	YE	HE	SE
O	TO	LO	KO	NO	MO	YO	HO	SO
U	TSU	LU	KU	NU	MU	YU	HU	SU

As you speak the consonants over and over, faster and faster, find your own rhythm. When you can do them by memory, close your eyes and sit in silence after ten minutes of practice and feel the electrical activation of the brain. Notice the difference between the Moon Order and the Sun Order. Your brain is receiving different signals because different neurological pathways are stimulated by each order.

For example, when working with the Sun Order TA LA KA NA MA YA HA SA... Saying these sounds as a mantra fixes in the body and subtle bodies everything that comes from the A dimension. In Kototama, the vibration of A represents the world of creativity, contemplative insight, and spiritual inspiration. We express this naturally when we say,"AH," upon entering a cathedral or seeing a beautiful star..

TCHI LI KI NI MI YI HI SI... This pattern integrates the totality of energy that is experienced with the first order, A, of consonants. I is the resonance representing the totality of all dimensions, the totality of energy. The energy and rhythm is more tight and dense than the energy of the first order.

TE LE KE NE ME YE HE SE... These sounds regenerate and discern all of the energy you have received. With the sword of clarity, which is the quality carried by the E dimension, that which is important is recognized and that which is not is discarded. The physical and subtle bodies vibrate with this energy. You are in touch with energy inside and out.

TO LO KO NO MO YO HO SO...activates deep memory and intellect, gives clarity to the brain and reinforces mental activity. According to Kototama, the sound O belongs to the mental realms and to the realms of cosmic memory.

TSU LU KU NU MU YU HU SU... This mantra is the Yoga of the cells. Because the vowel U represents physical energy, this mantra integrates all five dimensions into the body . The vowel U is linked with the physical senses.

In Kototama, vowels do not have the same sound as they do in English. A is pronounced AH, E is pronounced $\bar{A}$, I is pronounced $\bar{E}$, O is $\bar{O}$ as in English, U is OO as in boot.

Sound Practice II

This exercise represents a syntheses between acupuncture law and Kototama. The musical notes provided are the notes of the organ of the body which corresponds to the vowel sound. Therefore, the images and messages of the future Solar Time which arise are rooted in your biology. This connection assures that they are not merely mental concepts, but represents the coding in your cellular memory of future patterns. Sing the order of the Sun Time on the notes shown below.

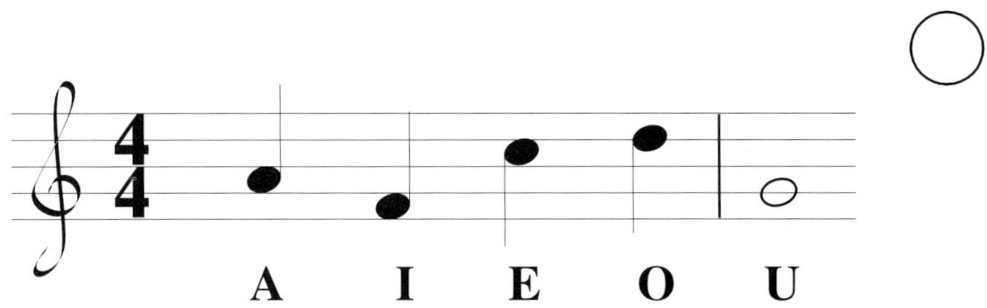

Next sing the Moon Time order: Sing repeatedly and let the resonance awaken Moon Time memories. The Old Knowledge still occupies a vibrational inner space in you, linked to the resonance of vowels sung in the Moon Order on the musical notes given.

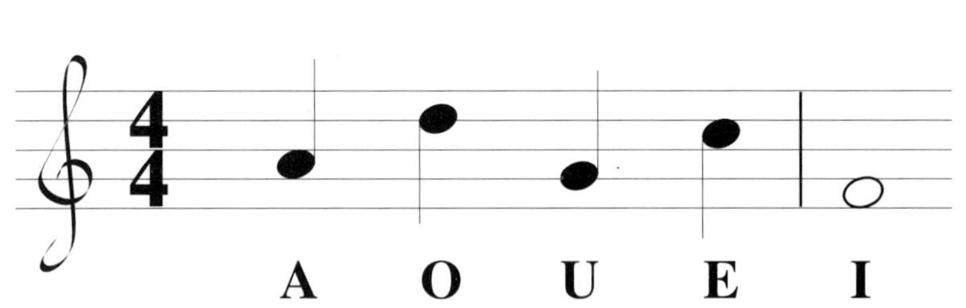

This exercise works best with a group of people. One half of the group sings the Sun Time Order answered by the other half singing the Moon Time order.

Working with Sound

When you work with sound, whether it is with the acoustic instruments of the five elements, overtones, the element sound of your voice, or the Kototama orders of vowels and consonants, you bypass the mental concepts and projections about what the resonance and messages of these teaching sounds should be and work directly with the vibrational source of inner and outer worlds.

It is important with each practice to develop your consciousness with the sound. If you are not "present," you may feel the energy, but have no awareness about where this energy really takes you, what it opens for you. With consciousness and practice, you begin to feel or hear the next sounds even before they come. This subtle ability is the signal that a link into higher consciousness has been created where you have access to new information.

Our natural inheritance is to become the multi-dimensional human being that, in truth, each of us is. As other dimensions of being open, you will find there are many more choices for artistic, scientific and soul expression available. You won't need to be educated as a scientist to understand sophisticated scientific theories, you won't need to be a professional musician to play or sing beautiful sounds. You will begin to have more moments when you are unified and aware of the many avenues of expression open to you.

The more you work with sound, the greater the chance to touch upon a specific frequency in resonance with a frequency in the brain or subtle body, which contains ancestral memories and cosmic messages. This information is essential to your life program.

Technique 8: Healing in the Subtle Bodies

Spiritual evolution has no end. It runs parallel to our physical development, continuing even after physical death. For example, the heart chakra is difficult for people to open - especially for those who are used to controlling their emotional karma and who cannot let go at this level. Nevertheless, the spiritual heart continues its development. If the human heart still resists at this time, strokes and heart attacks can be provoked. Since this process is applicable to all chakras, it is important to be aware of our own aura, or subtle bodies, before this phenomenon happens. Also, as explained in Book II, the health of the physical body depends directly upon the health of the subtle bodies.

In meditation we can come into resonance with our subtle bodies by raising our energy. There is a concentration of atoms in the structure of the physical and etheric body. As we progress farther and farther out, the density becomes more and more light; this is why we call these bodies "subtle." As the density becomes lighter, the spin of the atomic particles revolves faster and faster. Therefore it is more rare to see the farthest bodies such as the Buddhic and the Atmic. It is easier to see or sense the etheric and the astral which are more dense and vibrate more slowly.

Using Sound in the Subtle Bodies

Healing with sound in the subtle bodies is like "opening the silence" and listening to this silence. This type of healing involves tuning to your own silent dimensions as well as to those of your patient.

Sound in movement opens the perception of the subtle areas of energy when linked with the hara or Tantien. This work uproots from earth the energy to be channeled through the body and permits the link to the cosmic energy through the morphogenetic fields. Through this way we can change the resonance of our vibration.

Sound develops the psychic perception in the ear and makes the aura lighter. Sound as a meditation purifies the head and the thinking, eliminates interference and takes from the particles the heavy energy created by the vibration of the thinking. The sound enrobes the particles of vibration and causes them to expand by changing the spin (reversing the direction of rotation) of the particles. Thus, by changing their resonance, sound opens a new and wider field of consciousness.

Healing in the Subtle Bodies with Sound and Color

There are three different techniques used to heal the subtle bodies. They can be used separately or in combination.

1: Using singing bowls to harmonize the aura.

2: Scanning the wavelengths in three levels of the aura - etheric, astral and mental - and using sound and light to decrystallize negative concentrations in these subtle bodies.

3: Healing subtle bodies with acoustic musical instruments to clear the entire subtle body structure.

1: Using Singing Bowls to Harmonize the Aura

This technique heals the emotional body by balancing the astral body through the chakras. You can use Tibetan, Japanese or crystal bowls.

Sound the bowls from the feet to the head in the following progression of the Cycle of the Fifths: F C G D A E B
Some areas will absorb certain frequencies more than others. You will hear this discrepancy and know to ring this bowl for a longer time until the resonance coming back is equal among all the bowls.

The aura will be harmonized when the sound comes back to you right away, like an echo. When the sound has been completely absorbed or rejected, the harmonized aura will be full and vibrant.

After using the sound, you can have the patient use color glasses to fix the effect of the sound or just use orange and blue light to balance the general energy. At the end you can also use the monochord tuned with the key of the season.

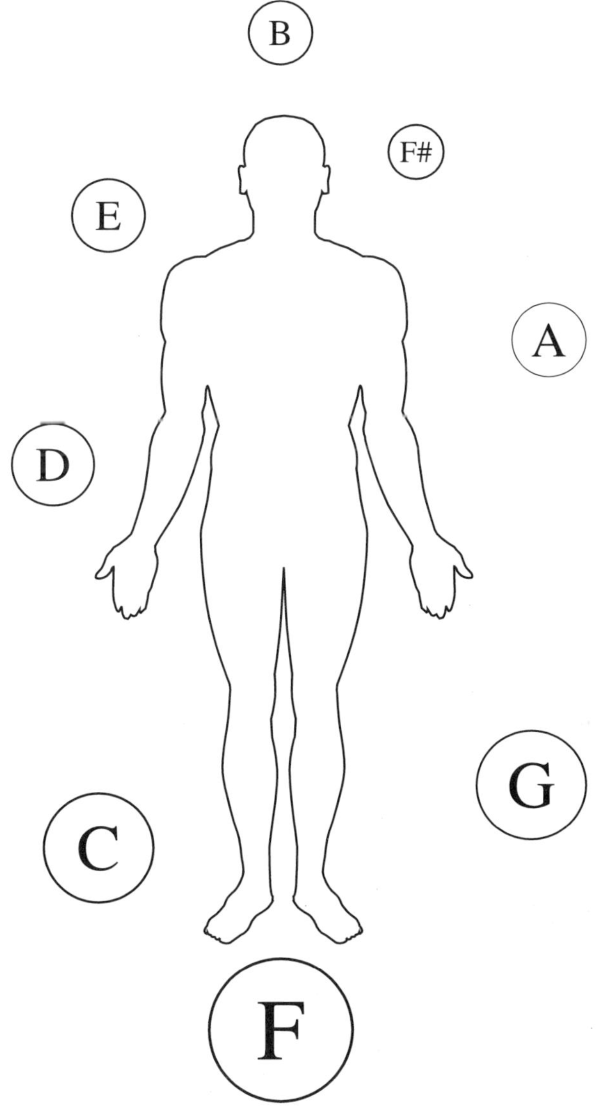

POSITIONS FOR HEALING BOWLS

2: Scanning Wavelengths on Three Levels

Scan layer by layer with your hand from the etheric level to the highest subtle body that you can feel, starting at the patient's feet each time. Notice at each level the area of crystallization of energy in the fields. You will end up finding several points of crystallization of energy in the different subtle body layers. If you connect these points with an imaginary line you will see the form of the wavelength disturbing the patient. This line could have many symbolically significant shapes that you know and some that you don't know, such as forms of letters from ancient languages like Arabic, Sanskrit, Hebrew, Celtic or Aramaic, perhaps linked with the original ancestry of the patient.

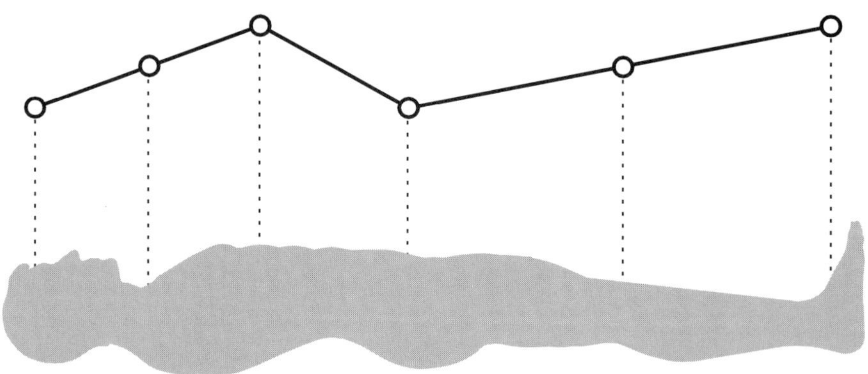

This wavelength will create a geometric projection of its energy into the physical energy below. For example, you can end up with a waveform like the one shown in the preceding picture.

Next you can use an instrument for its appropriate five element quality in the right frequency to diminish the adherence of the crystallization of perverse energy in the aura.

The instruments to use are as follows:

			Key of
EARTH	from the feet to the coccyx	ocarina	F
WATER	hara area	water drum, drum	C
WOOD	in the solar plexus area liver - spleen	wood flute, wood percussion	G
FIRE	in the heart area	strings, monochord	D
AIR/METAL	lungs,thymus, throat	gong, bells, silver balls, silver flute	A
ETHER	for head and beyond	all little sounds: Chinese balls Rain stick	E
		Overtone created by natural elements such as wind	B

After using the sound, use the white light on each point of the waveform you found in the aura and then along the entire wavelength to erase any trace of crystallization of negative energy and to complete the effect of the sound.

3. Healing Subtle Bodies with Acoustic Instruments

There are three main musical progressions to consider for healing with acoustic instruments. The first for the **physical body** follows the organ structure with the specific tonality and instruments linked with acupuncture using the **fundamental note for each meridian**. (see "Tuning Forks on the Shu Points" technique).

The second musical progression for the **astral body** follows the chakra structure using the **musical Cycle of Fifths:** F C G D A E B and is used for healing the emotional body.

The third musical progression works in the **subtle bodies** from **the etheric** to the **Atmic** body following the **overtone progression** in the aura.

Healing in the subtle bodies creates a positive effect in the physical body because imbalances are created first in the aura and duplicated later in the physical body. The pure sound of the acoustic instruments of the elements of nature clarifies the aura. This opens a new space of consciousness, allowing the resonance of the ancestral memories into the present through the central axis.

For healing in the subtle bodies you can follow the overtone progression with a special range of instruments used for the subtle bodies from the etheric to the Atmic. Begin with the note F, the tonality of the earth surface frequency, and build from there.

With acoustic instruments, the progression is followed with the appropriate instrument and tonality. Maintain a separation of seven seconds between each instrument to allow for the breathing of the subtle bodies.

This separation of seven seconds is the duration of resonance which is necessary in order to have access from level to level without disturbing the energy (as in meditation).

In the subtle bodies, from the etheric to the Atmic body, follow the overtone progression by zone. As you move from the feet to the head in the space of the aura, sound the progression of the Cycle of Fifths, the fundamental scale which works in the subtle bodies, by zone, using the respective musical instrument as shown in the chart.

This specific progression helps open up the energy of consciousness, giving access to different realms of the deep memory and allowing the release of tension inherent to each level. Just listening to the recording of this sequence will aid this transformation.[18]

In subtle body healing it is important to place your instruments in a way that does not cut the field or space of the patient. Move as little and as efficiently as possible whenever you need to access an instrument.

Musical Progression for Healing Physical and Subtle Bodies

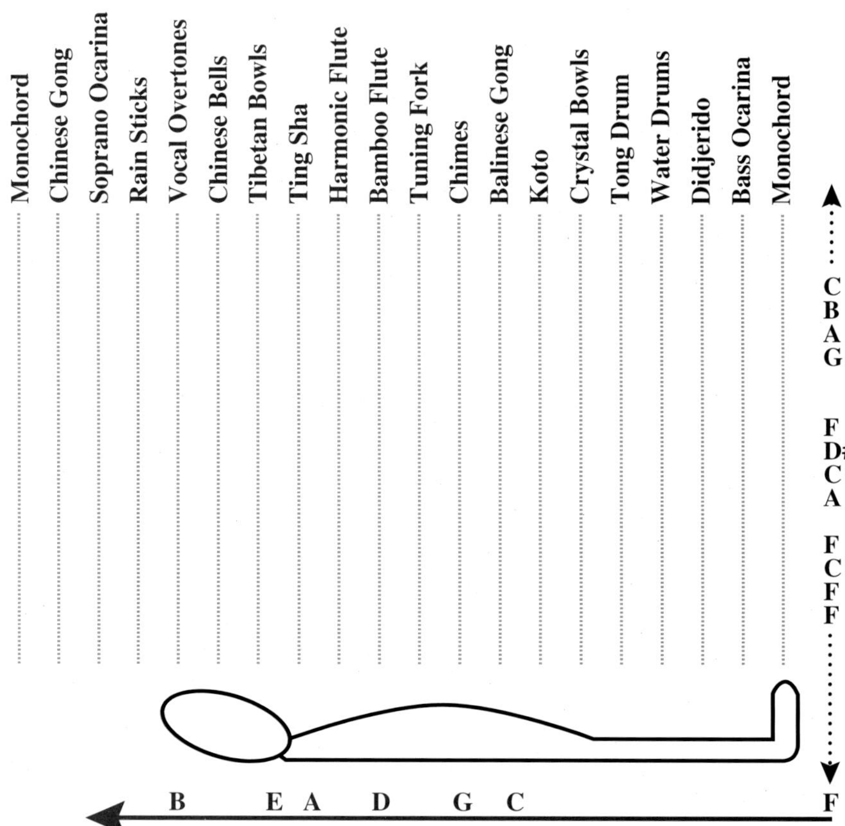

After the sound, use color quintessences to open to the highest dimension of nature linked with the Devas.[19]

Technique 9

A: The Sefirotic Tree
The Crystal Sound Healing Structure

B: The Sefirotic Tree and the Chinese Temperaments

A: The Sefirotic Tree

The Stages of Life

The Sefirotic Tree, or Tree of Life, was originally a model which described different initiatic stages, psychological states or pathways through which human beings pass at various stages during the course of a lifetime. Each of the Ten Sefirot represents a specific state of psychological and spiritual development.

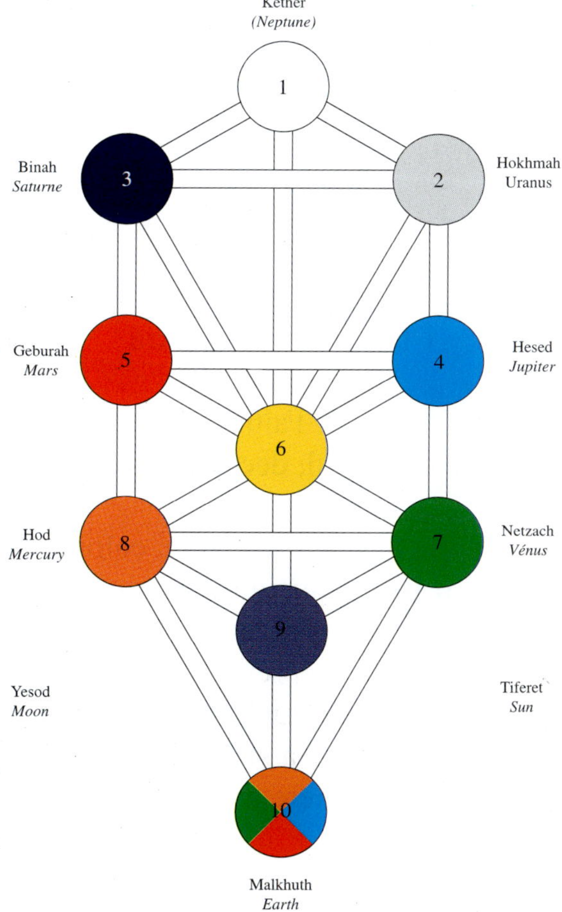

Description of the Ten Sefirot

1. KETHER

Level: Spiritual
Chakra: Crown
Planet: Neptune
Characteristics: Awareness, God's Will, Cosmic Consciousness,
I Am that I Am, accomplishment, serenity, experience of wonder

The test of the Tree of Life evolves from this stage. This is the First Incarnation, the source of our divine identity. Through Kether we enter existence and connect with Malkhuth for grounding. Kether can be accessed only through Binah and Hokhmah. Kether is the source and of creation of non-manifested death; what is and what is not.

2. HOKHMAH

Level: Spiritual
Chakra: Sixth Chakra
Planet: Uranus
Characteristics: Divine Will, Faithful Father, power, discipline,
wisdom, sexual symbol, decision, deep knowledge

From Hokhmah we can see through structure, color and sound. Hokhmah is the will of creation. It is a demanding energy, a "must do it" energy. This stage affects the kidneys. Its energy is represented as pure wisdom transmitted by spirit. Hokhmah represents wisdom which is a vibratory presence or reality, not just conceptual. The energy of Hokhmah speaks through, not to. Hokhmah carries a strong will that lets you know what to do and that you must do it. There are no lies and no alternatives possible.

3. BINAH

Level: Spiritual
Chakra: Sixth
Planet: Saturn
Characteristics: Mother Nature, Divine Heart, acceptance, intuition, femininity, priestess, the inner voice

Binah represents compassion, the ability to accept ourselves as we are. Binah removes the fear of being open; it is understanding which opens the soul. The energy of Binah facilitates the acceptance of duality and when one accepts duality, there is no longer duality. This is not a stage for testing, there is just openness and acceptance at the level of Binah. Binah prepares us for Hokhmah. It is the first manifestation of form. It concretizes shape at the spiritual level. Binah represents complete understanding and acceptance of all archetypes in the unconscious. This Sefira could be called the Akashic ocean of consciousness. People who work with magic and with star energies work here. Binah puts us in contact with the stars and with their archetypal representations (such as the Big Dipper's link with the Round Table, the Little Dipper's link with the Holy Grail).

4. HESED

Level: Mental
Chakra: Throat (Fifth Chakra)
Planet: Jupiter
Characteristics: Mercy, kindness, benevolence, compassion, human greatness, pure love

Mercy and understanding through feeling reflect the religious resonance of this Sefira. Hesed represents the protective aspect of love. Because Hesed does not ignore the roots of a person, it offers grounding on the spiritual path. The higher one goes in spirit, the more grounding is necessary. When combined with Geburah, Hesed brings the beginning of the experience of individuality. Hesed corresponds to the mental subtle body.

5. GEBURAH

Level: Mental
Chakra: Throat (Fifth Chakra)
Planet: Mars
Characteristics: Judgment, severity, discipline, Divine Decree, Divine Duty, rule, duty, efficiency, Divine Warrior, strictness

Geburah defends the respect for the law and represents a necessary step in spiritual development. Here one can escape or transcend emotion and enter into the mental level. However, if Geburah is not modified by the Sefira, Tiferet, there is the risk of becoming lost in the mental aspect. The danger is that the mental can be used as an escape. The lesson is to understand why one is escaping.

6. TIFERET

Level: Astral and Mental
Chakra: Heart (Fourth Chakra)
Planet: Sun
Characteristics: Innocence of a Child, harmony, beauty, purity, sensitivity of the senses

Tiferet is the blessed, innocent child. The adult in us needs this child within. Here we accept all things in a childlike way. There are many paths to this level, which represents the solar plexus in line with the fire of the heart. There is a rebirth process when the inner child has been found.

When we return to the child, we have no protection. We lose the ability to protect ourselves and need guidance to integrate this childlike innocence. Here the programming is not set in place. This is a resting place between the astral and the mental. Tiferet brings unconditional, non-emotional, unattached love. There is balance with this energy. When an adult discovers Tiferet, the second birth is begun.

7. NETZACH

Level: Astral
Chakra: Solar Plexus (Third Chakra)
Planet: Moon
Characteristics: Beautiful lady, emotional enjoyment, virtue, transmutation, joy, artistic ability, cultural consciousness, soft seduction, play, linked with freedom of nature

Ntzah represents victory without force, the eternal victory of love. Netzach creates love through emotion and also carries the seduction of beauty. The victory is the transformation of physical desire into pure love. Netzach lifts energy up. Hawaii is the Netzach of the United States.

8. HOD

Level: Astral
Chakra: Solar Plexus (Third Chakra)
Planet: Mercury
Characteristics: Practical and Pragmatic Wisdom, humor, adaptability, the glory of genius, mind over matter, honor, flexibility, perception, clever.

Hod is the masculine aspect of Netzach. It is initiated intelligence, representing the Aikido of the mind. It is a mercurial energy. Hod is the consciousness of truth, working from the middle brain. It provides a quick processing of information.

9. YESOD

Level: Astral
Chakra: Sexual (Second Chakra)
Planet: Moon
Characteristics: Foundations of universe, virility, psychic, genetics, male, sexual stability, sexual activity, respectful, reproduction, shamanic, solid-etheric, domain of personal unconscious.

Yesod gives life to what can be born. It is the hidden aspect of creation. In combination with Malkhuth, the elements of wood and fire are activated. Yesod is the marriage of the lower part of civilization. Almost 90 to 95% of humanity is at the level of Yesod and Malkhuth. The remaining percentage of humanity which has reached a higher level of consciousness feels the heaviness of these two levels and the sadness of the soul for where the others are.

Yesod gives a clear vision of life and the means to organize the structure of subtle energy into matter. Yesod gives life for Mother Earth to give birth just as the Divine Sun and Moon give birth to Mother Earth.

Yesod represents creativity at the spiritual level, the transmutation of sexual energy into etheric power and into matter. Yesod controls sexual energy. It holds the key to feeling the differences between the material and non-material worlds. Magical experiences which come from the moon and etheric energy occur here.

Around the age of thirty five, life changing events occur within a seven year period. They are experienced almost as cosmic, magical events and they help to move one along on the spiritual path.

Clairvoyance and clairaudience reside in Yesod. It is this level through which the angelic realm works, but awareness is needed in order to access the angelic. The movement of medical research to more subtle therapies is occurring through Yesod.

The influence of the moon on all liquids on earth resides here. Yesod, carrying etheric energies, is directly linked with the nervous system, meridians, and then the blood system. The etheric body contains the programs and images of the physical life and we are able to change them through shape, vibration and symbol changes.

Without the moon, which is resident in Yesod, we have no access to our psychic abilities. Therefore, Yesod holds the key to understanding the life of the physical and the psychic. The moon receives the light from the sun which comes from the Divine. Shamans use the hidden (reflective) power of the moon. To influence moon energy, use chi, music and meditation. Yesod creates the stability of the genetic organs in the body. It links magic and the etheric.

10. MALKHUTH

Level: Physical
Chakra: Root (First Chakra)
Planet: Earth
Characteristics: Feminine, newborn, womb, water and earth, birth and death, world, density, collective unconscious, roots of archetzpes, roots of life.

Malkuth represents the age of either death or illumination. We cannot see the Divine from here. Malkhuth resonates with Yesod. It is the kingdom of nature and Mother Earth, where the woman initiates the behavior in man. Malkhuth is the feminine aspect, the yin. It is acceptance. If Malkhuth is not open, the male or yang aspect cannot enter into life, for the yang actions are based on the opening of the yin.

Malkhuth is the physical body. It is the deep storage of the mystical way. The divine expression through life resides here. The message of spirit resides in the bones. The skeleton remains after death as the witness of the divine on earth. The divine fire resides in the bones as the breathing of the bone marrow (neidan). Malkhuth holds the chemical movement of chi. It is the mystical marriage of the divine and matter in the DNA. From the divine marriage comes the nobility of nature. Disciplines such as Chi Gong and yoga help the chi reach the bones. Malkuth allows the expression of the Divine in nature. The astral power enters through the etheric. Our desire and will reside in the astral, are integrated into the etheric and then into the physical.

Malkhuth holds hidden knowledge and information. We cannot evolve beyond Malkhuth through escape; we move beyond Malkhuth through consciousness and awareness.

The fastest way to move beyond Malkhuth is through the practice of Chinese chi exercises which nourish the etheric body. Without etheric energy, the nervous system of the body cannot remain strong.

The cosmic doctrines of Madame Blavatsky and Alice Bailey state that each conscious individual lives to die and dies to live. It is through death that we gather the fruit of life. We are like cows that eat the grass of the earth and afterward lay down on the field of the sky to ruminate about what we did before in our lives.

Death is the meditation of the soul. After this lifetime, we will meditate in our soul until our next lifetime. Malkhuth, the bridge between life and death, earth and sky, also carries the consciousness of matter. Most of our difficulties are concerned with moving beyond Malkhuth and Yesod. These are the two most important levels of growth.

Description of the Twenty-Two Pathways of the Sefirotic Tree

PERSONALITY

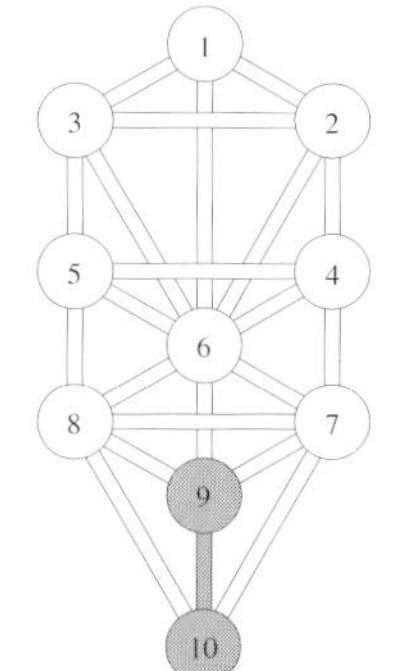

32. Malkhuth ➛ Yesod
Tarot = XXI
Astrology = Saturn
Hebrew = Daath - The Cross
Age = 0-7

This pathway represents the main etheric polarity of sexuality. The underground of the subconscious flows through Yesod and transforms into creativity. If Malkhuth is out of balance, we do not form the etheric connection, and our creativity does not form. Creativity is a manifestation of devotion. This pathway could lead to the mystical way. The lesson here is to learn the existence of causality as we ascend from Malkhuth to Yesod. To do one thing creates something else. There are more subtle and important things than mere physical matter. This pathway represents our first awareness. We descend from Kether to Malkhuth to learn the excitation ofthe limitation of spirit by dense matter. We have to accept this limitation or we cannot incarnate. We usually go via pathway 32 first to connect with the energy of the etheric. If contact with the etheric energy is not made, we will die. This contact is generally made sometime from birth to age seven.

29. Malkhuth ➛ Netzach
Tarot: XVIII - The Moon
Astrology: Pisces
Hebrew: Kof - The Head

This is the pathway that helps for the development of Malkhuth. Way 29 is linked with heredity, biology and instincts. Netzach awakens the sexuality of Malkhuth. This pathway creates physical reproduction. It is connected with female, moon and blood. One of symbols of this pathway is the labia. Way 29 is represented by the goddesses Aphrodite and Isis, symbols of beauty and seduction and magnifies femininity of matter and body. This path is more concerned with the expression of beauty, rather than the desire to attract. If family pressure suppresses this expression, this way can be difficult. This phase usually occurs before the age of twenty, primarily between the ages of seven through fourteen.

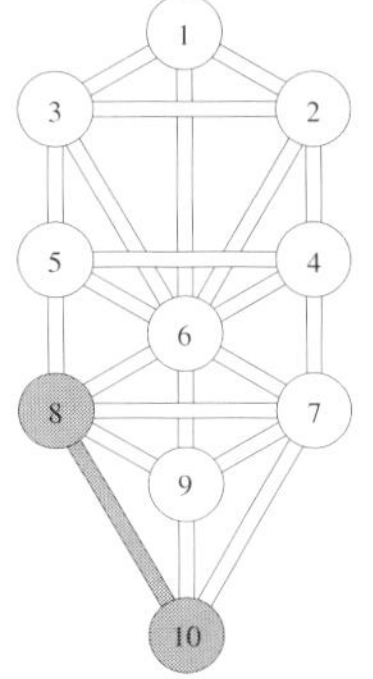

31 Malkhuth ➛ Hod
Tarot: XX - judgment
Astrology: Primal fire
Hebrew: Shin - Teeth

This pathway represents the perpetual intelligence of mind. Its symbols are the moon and sun, yin and yang. It is the primal fire from the earth which develops into the creative intelligence and artistic part of humanity. It brings together the more feminine (Malkhuth) to the masculine (Hod). Because the pathway comes from Malkhuth, it represents the more earthy development of the artistic. For family, it is the opportunity to raise children in an artistic way.

Way 31 reveals the possibilities of Malkhuth and Hod to pull out the best creative possibilities of matter. This path can be suppressed in families who do not know how to nurture the artistic. Religion has been responsible for suppressing much of the energy of pathways 29-30-31. Until we reach Tiferet, our full creativity cannot be expressed. Before reaching Tiferet, we still have the ability to repair any imbalances in the lower paths. Most people are able to repair themselves unless a total suppression has occurred. Hyperactive children are the result of the suppression of Yesod-Netzach, which directs all energy to Hod. Sexual abuse is usually the result of suppression of Way 29. To heal 29-31-32, it is necessary to bring in beauty. As we move to Tiferet, fear disappears.

28 Yesod ➣ Netzach
Tarot: IV - The Emperor
Astrology: Aquarius
Hebrew: Tzaddi-Hook

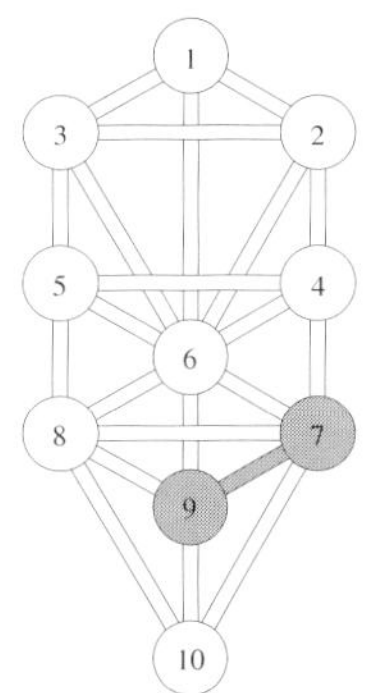

This path provides the structure of the personality. It is the way of material intelligence. All things under the sun will be understood perfectly. Etheric flow and chi flow reside here. In this path rests intuition, desire, strength and pure creativity. There are no limitations. Here is the channel of artistic and scientific inspiration. There is always the danger that the highest inspirations can degenerate into sexual obsession because this path works with etheric sexuality. Art loves beauty, but with an underlying sexuality. This is part of our unconscious.

30 Yesod ➣ Hod
Tarot: XIX - The Sun
Hebrew: Resh-Head (Brain)

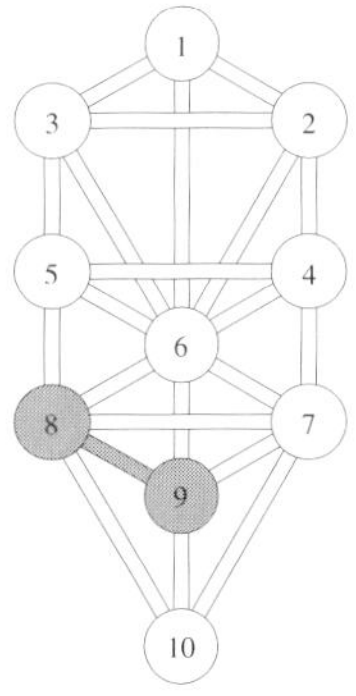

This is the path of creative intelligence, not the personal conscious mind. It possesses the knowledge of the stars, the clearance for all divinity and all wisdom of the stars and planets. It brings a collective sense of the whole scale of the strength of each level as they interconnect. It connects with the superior beings of light who are the Ascended Masters. This is the path through which we move beyond pain and suffering into higher consciousness. It lifts humanity to the Divine. The main suffering of humanity is that the self feels unworthy to be in the presence of God.

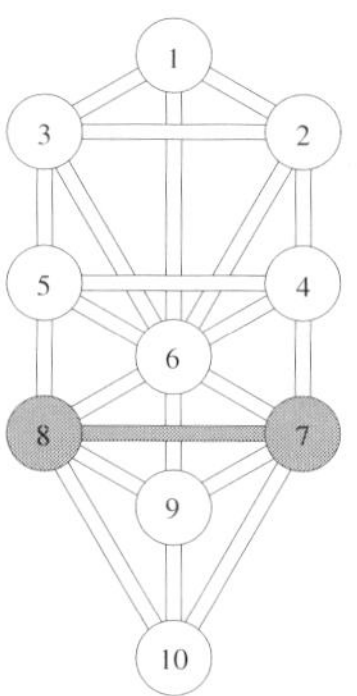

27 Hod ➛ Netzach
Tarot = XVI House of God
Astrology. Mars
Hebrew = Peh - Mouth

This is an active path which receives the movement of spirit. There is basic support for the personality, for the mind and for creativity. The lesson here is how to find the balance between the left and right brain. The test is to raise yourself up, rather than falling back. If one falls back to Yesod, there is still the free will or choice to center in mind or center in feeling.

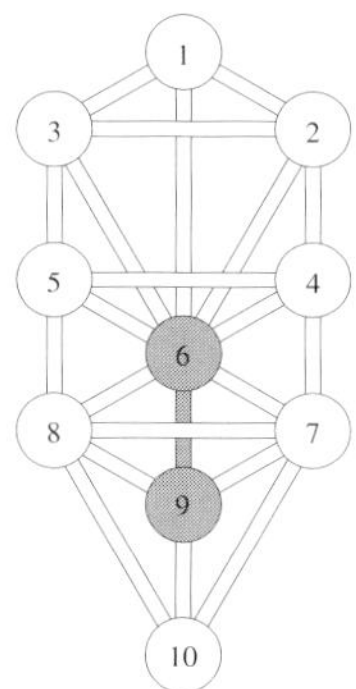

25 Yesod ➛ Tiferet
Tarot = XIV - Temperance
Astrology = Sagittarius
Hebrew = Samech - Sustenance, support

This path represents the temptation of Divine will. Here those who are afraid to go up , go down instead. Many fail on this path. With success one can pass here from the personality to individuality. Attachment to the physical can be released.

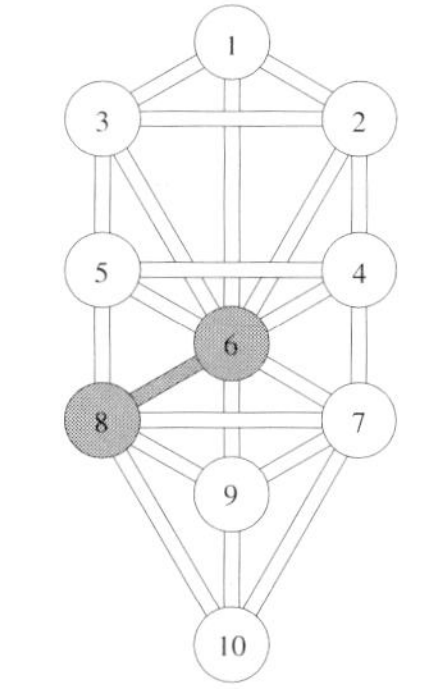

26 Hod ➛ Tiferet
Tarot: XV - The Devil
Astrology: Capricorn
Hebrew: Fa - Eyes

This path represents the renewing of intelligence. The Divine renews all structure through the regeneration of the sun. All of our past builds our structure. We reconnect with the eyes of a child and see through to the past. This perspective brings new light to the structure. It is necessary to see with the eyes of a child. If we cannot, we fall back to Hod. This regression happens when too much time is spent dwelling upon the past. It is also the result of being too hard and too inflexible. We must let go of the mental. Chi exercises and meditation are the best tools for developing this ability.

24 Netzach ➛ Tiferet
Tarot: XIII - Death
Astrology: Scorpio
Hebrew: Nun-Fish

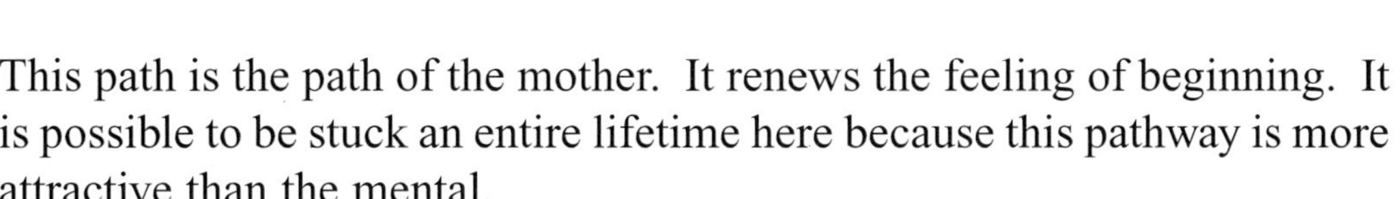

This path is the path of the mother. It renews the feeling of beginning. It is possible to be stuck an entire lifetime here because this pathway is more attractive than the mental.

Ways 24-26 are difficult transitions because it is possible to be trapped in the lower triangles, recreating continuously these three pathways. It will seem as if you are making progress, but, in reality, you will be only creating illusion.

INDIVIDUALITY

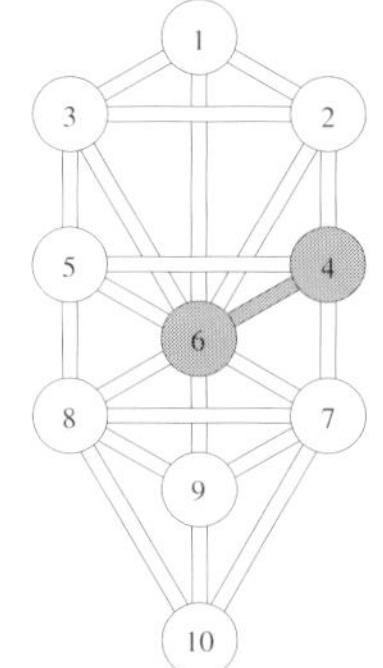

20. Tiferet ➛ Hesed
Tarot: IX - Hermit
Astrology: Virgo
Hebrew: Addend

This is the path that begins the move out of the sphere of personality into the sphere of individuality. This path brings the intelligence of will, the possibility of preparation. Everything and every being is created by will. From will, we then arrive at compassion. This is the phase which contains the knowledge of primal wisdom. Now God can see all. This path accepts all and loves all without judgment. We must exercise more will to prepare to accept higher wisdom. Children are good teachers for Ways 20 and 22.

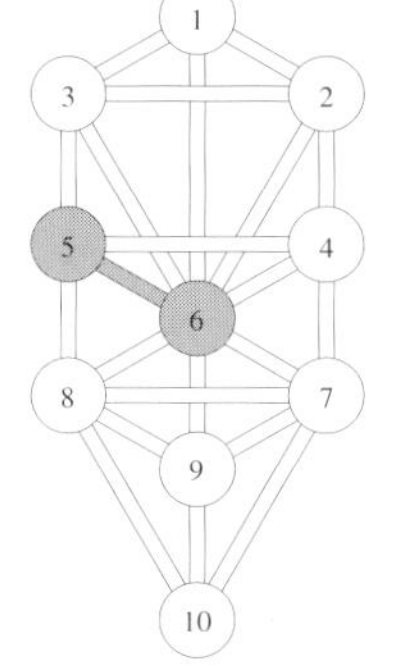

22 Tiferet ➛ Geburah
Tarot: VII - Justice
Hebrew: Lamed - Cattle, produce

This is the path of the good, obedient soldier. It represents faithfulness to duty and order from the Divine. This energy may appear as stubborn. The danger of this path is that it is easy to become lost in detail and forget one's purpose. Maintaining spiritual quality is difficult here because of the power of the energy. We must prod without being aggressive. Discernment is imperative here or we revert to judgment. Once we have reached this level, we cannot fall all the way back to the lower levels; we can only go back to Tiferet and "play."

19 Geburah ➛ Hesed
Tarot: XI - Strength
Astrological: Leo
Hebrew: Teth - Serpent, snake

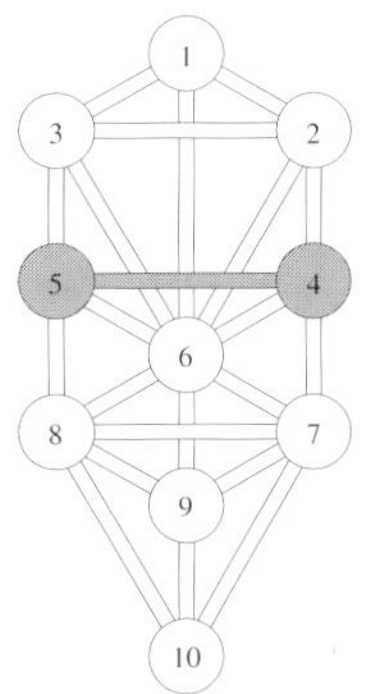

This is the path which contains the intelligence of all secret activity of the spiritual beings who work without being known. It is the place of exalted feelings, compassion and the best guardian of heaven. This is where we learn to work separately together. We must be able to keep deep secrets because they belong to the universe, not to humanity. If we are given a message from the Divine, we must keep silent until the time is appropriate to reveal its message. We need the strength to be silent.

21. Netzach ➛ Hesed
Tarot: X - Wheel of Fortune
Astrology: Jupiter
Hebrew: Kadh - Palm of hand

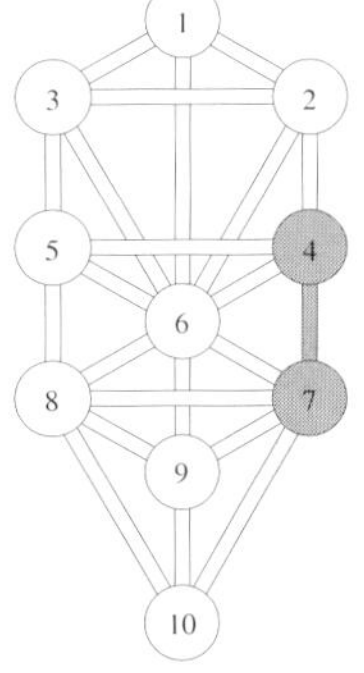

This is the intelligence of reconciliation, coming together. It represents the influence of blessing and benediction. Here the personality is overwhelmed by blessing.

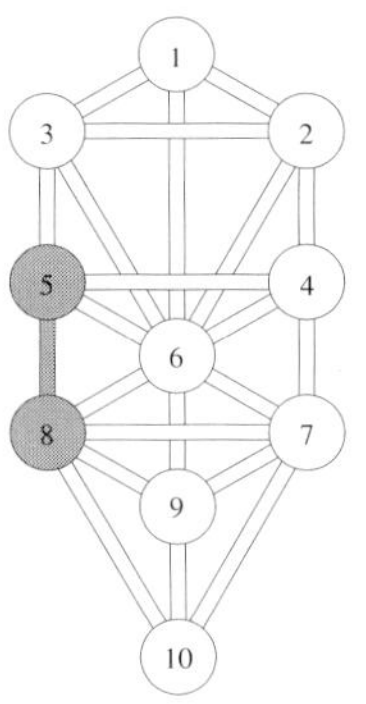

23 Hod ➛ Geburah
Tarot: XII - Hanged Man
Astrology: Water
Hebrew: Mem - Water

This is the place of stable intelligence and coherence. It is like two minds, one containing structure (Geburah) and one containing intuition (Hod). This gift is distributed to all beings on earth when they are ready. It is necessary to work with chi or meditation in order to feel this energy. It is the transformation level of the body to the mind.

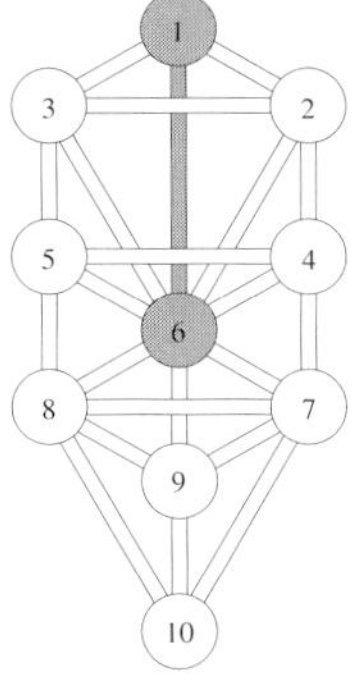

SPIRITUAL
13 Tiferet ➛ Kether
Tarot: High Priestess
Astrology: Moon
Hebrew: Gimel - Camel

This is the path of unifying intelligence. It contains the light and essence of glory. This pathway is the perfection and truth of everything spiritual. It is the feeling that exists beyond blessing.

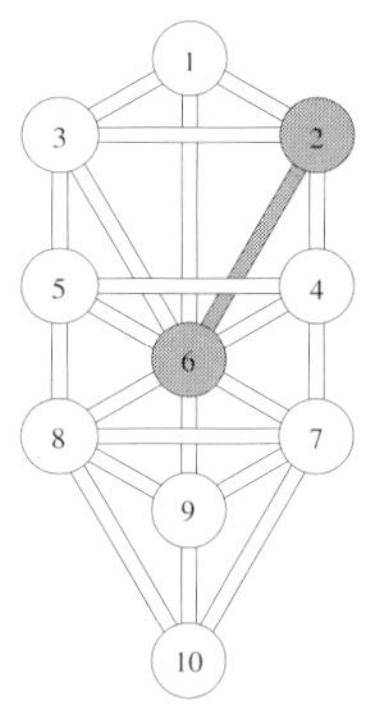

15 Tiferet ➛ Hokhmah
Tarot: VI - Lover
Astrology: Gemini
Hebrew: Heh - Window

This path represents the hidden God. Pathway 15 is the intelligence of transformation beginning in the body through sensation and continuing through emotion into concept. Here we transmute and move into total acceptance. Beyond concept, we face the vision on higher levels through the fusion of understanding. We learn to face the light beings and vision.

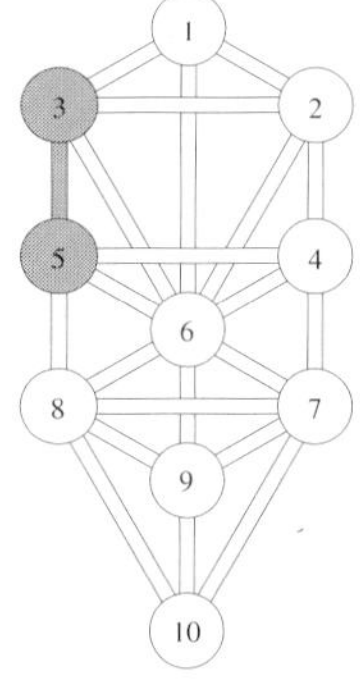

18 Geburah ➛ Binah
Tarot: VII - Chariot
Astrology: Cancer
Hebrew: Cheth - Fence

This pathway represents the intelligence of the home of influence. The greatness expressed through Geburah distributes an abundance of good until all beings on earth are satisfied. On this pathway we are able to receive the creation of Divine. It possesses the blessing of the universe to all beings.

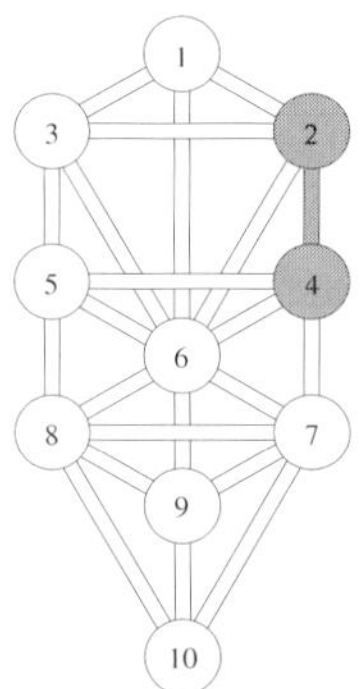

16 Hesed ➛ Hokhmah
Tarot = V - Pope
Astrology = Taurus
Hebrew = Jau - Nail

Here we reach triumph and internal intelligence. Path 16 offers the pleasure of glory beyond which there is no equal. The structure of spirit is revealed on this pathway.

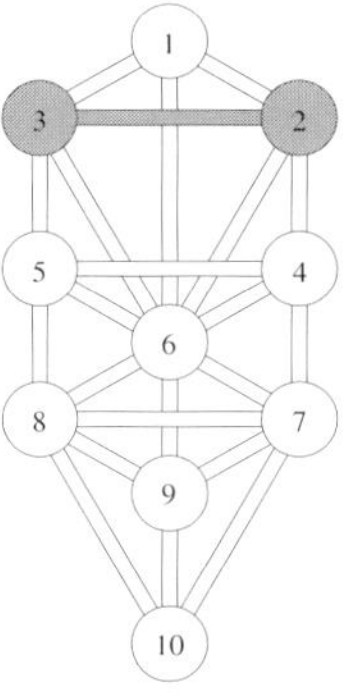

14 Binah ➛ Hokhmah
Tarot = III - Empress
Astrological = Venus
Hebrew = Daleth - Door

Path 14 represents illuminated intelligence. It contains the axis of the founder of the hidden idea of saintedness in the phase of preparation. This pathway is associated with canonization. Here is found the first will and first acceptance of Divine. Path 14 is both male and female energies.

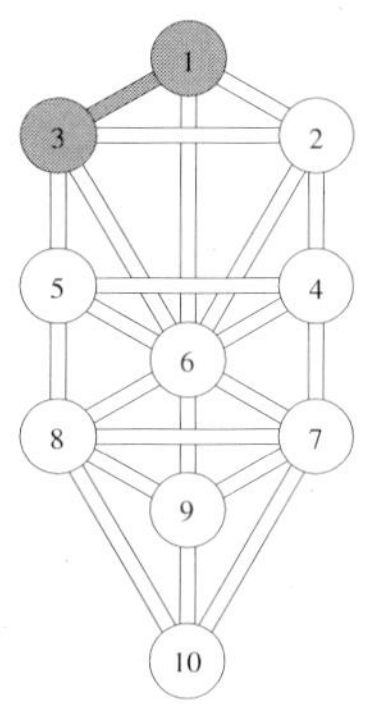

12 Binah ➛ Kether
Tarot = I - Magician
Astrological = Mercury
Hebrew = Beth - Home

This pathway symbolizes the intelligence of transparence. It requires the capacity to see things of the world as the really are. The shape/form of things cannot be hidden from this light. To those on this pathway, the light of God is revealed, not hidden.

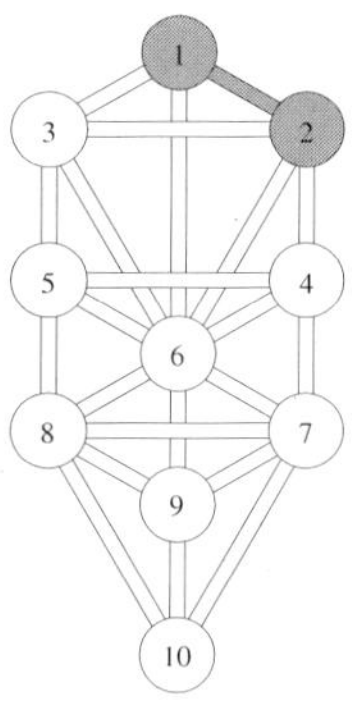

11 Hokhmah ➛ Kether
Tarot = O - Fool
Astrology = Ether/Air/Fire
Hebrew = Aleph - Bull

This is the path of shining intelligence. It is the essence of the veil placed beyond all creation and reality. A special dignity is given to those on this pathway making it possible to stand in front of God.

THE TREE OF LIFE

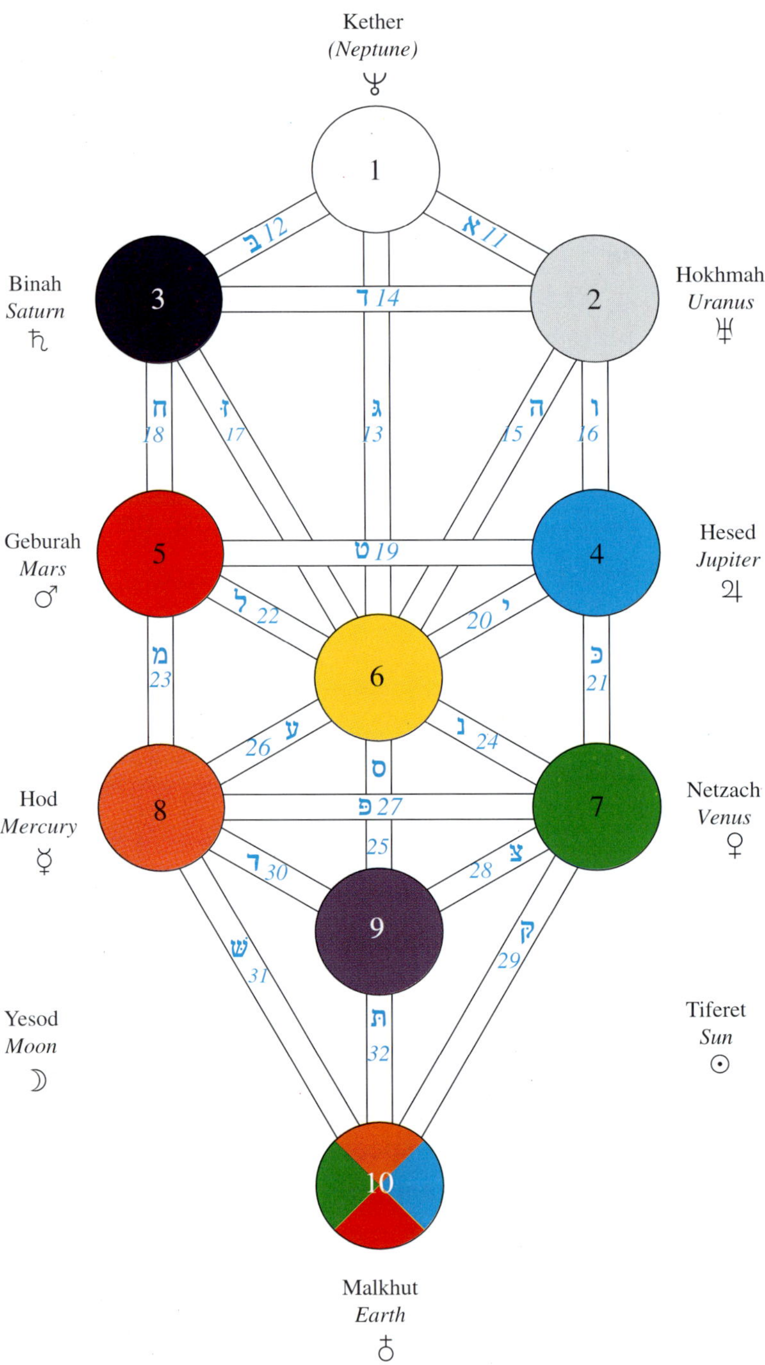

THE QUALITIES OF THE SEFIROT

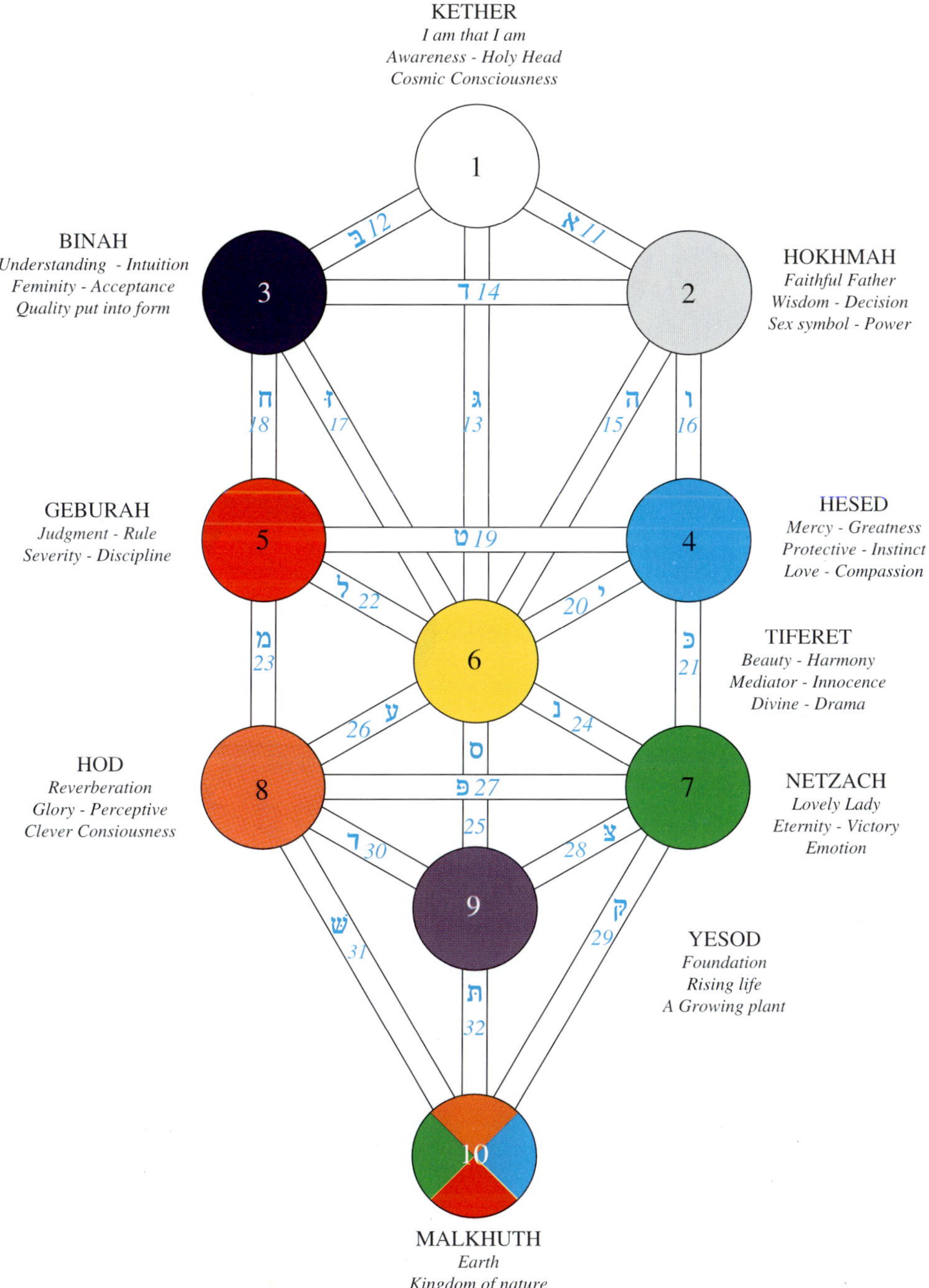

The Element fire in the Sefirotic Tree corresponds
to the Divine Fire represented by the three Divine Ethers, Binah, Hokhmah, Kether.
The other three elements correspond to the normal chakra progression earth, water, air.
Daath, the Divine Mirror corresponds to Alta Major,
the hidden chakra, source of pure consciousness.
(Bindu in the Indian tradition).

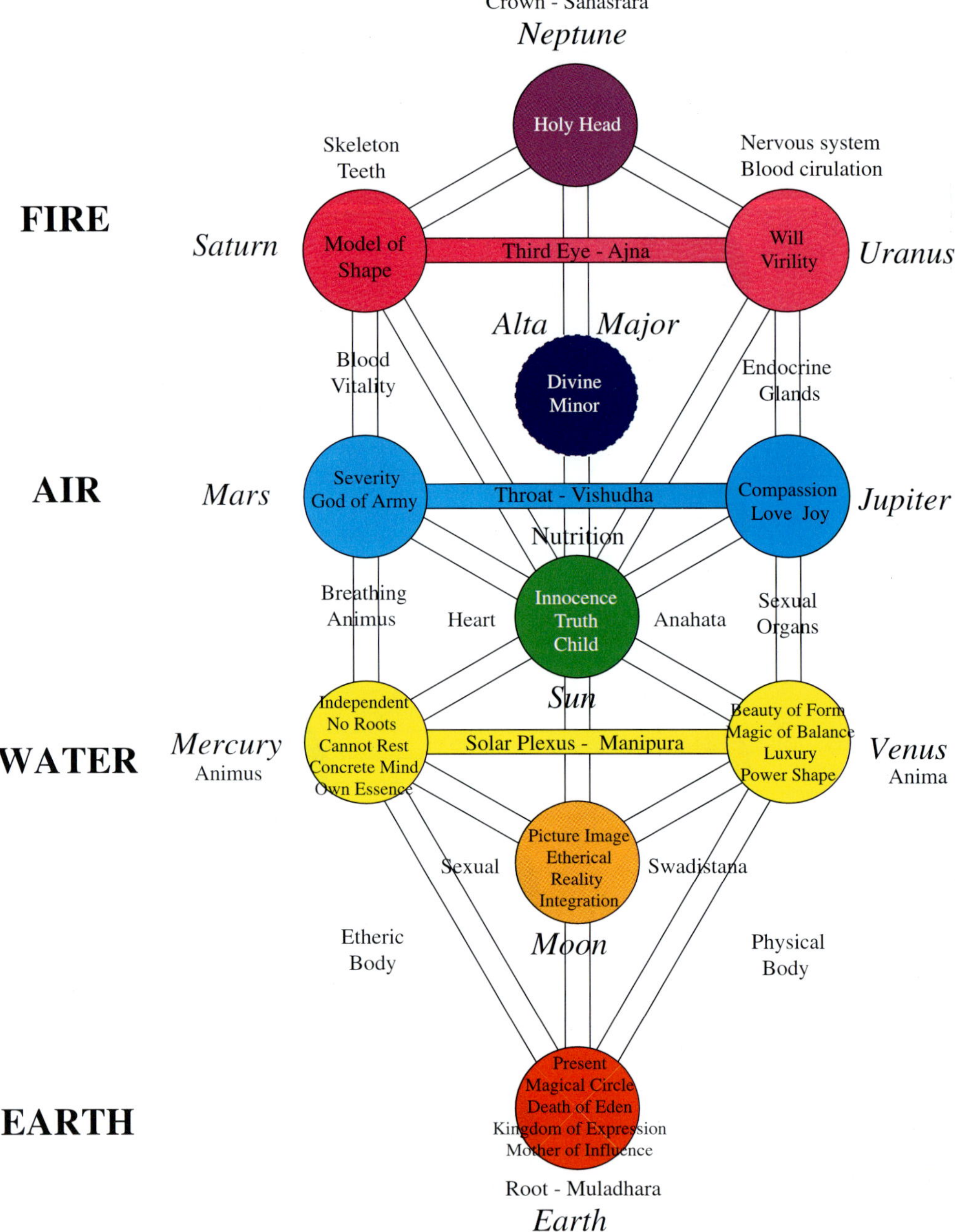

The four functions of Jungian psychology are linked with the four Sefirot
Tiferet = Intuition
Netzach = Sentiment
Hod = Thinking
Malkhuth = Sensation

CHAKRAS AND SEFIROT

INNER CORRESPONDENCE

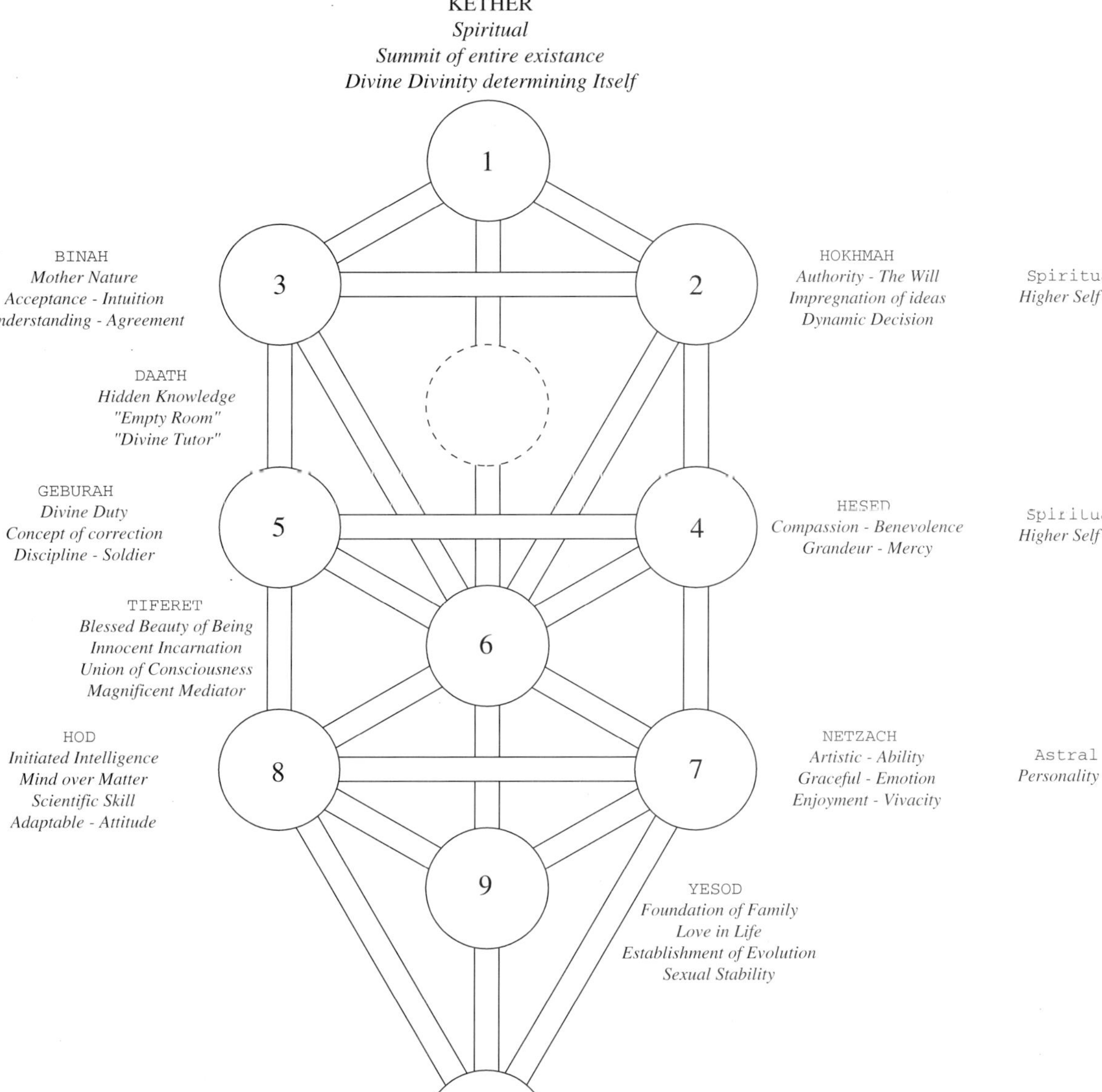

MALKHUTH
Mystical Marriage with Matter
Nobility of Nature
Perfect Partner for Material Man
Human Hope
Emancipation from Earth

Physical
Body

Sefirotic Tree and the Crystal Healing Structure

As I worked with sound and movement and chi in physical, astral/emotional and mental level, I wondered how to work on the spiritual levels with also natural elements.

When I studied the Sefirotic structure of the Kaballah, I understood that we could work also through this structure using sound, crystal and light and even effect the DNA. Here we work as far as we can with the light of the sun, awakening the crystal energy. The sound reactivates the light energy through the crystal and helps the integration of the exact quality of energy needed in the subtle and physical bodies.

I use fine crystal spheres hung in a structure of the Sefirotic Tree which faces the body as shown in the chart. The light of the sun is reflected through the crystal sphere in front of each appropriate zone of the body. At the same time master tubes in the frequencies of the different Sefira are sounded.

The patient is in a meditative state and both healer and patient are tuned with the light energy which guides the session. This process involves an exquisite structure and process of healing and is experienced as a meditative transformation.

The sound of the hanging tubes reactivates the power of each crystal sphere which opens its intelligence and channels to the rays of the light of the sun. The sun opens a part of the spectrum of color in each crystal sphere which will enter the body. The geometric shape hanging in front of the standing physical body completes the experience by integrating all the different levels of energy through the resonance of the sound.

Each person receives exactly the right intensity and the right amount of energy needed to readjust his or her entire energy in the moment. Though there is a result in the physical level, the main alignment takes place in the subtle bodies (linked with the karma and Dharma of each person).

Here is a method where the healer has no interaction in the healing process. Healing occurs through the spirit of the elements which are directly in contact with the patient.

It is almost as if the healing is offered by the Devas, the spiritual nature of the elements. The only action the healer takes is to ring the appropriate sound for each person. It is extremely important to respect the individual timing of each person's ability to remain standing between the crystals and the sound in order not to confuse the subtle bodies. (One should never stay more than one minute in front of the structure).

Crystal Healing Structure

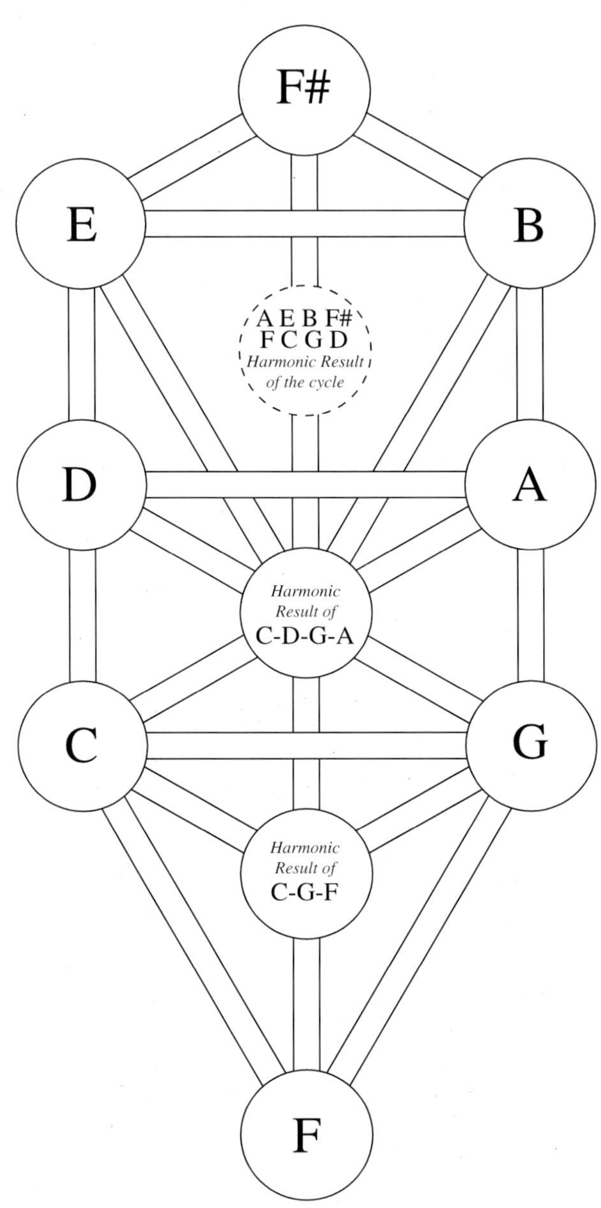

SOUND AND THE SEFIROTIC TREE

Sound Crystal Healing Structure

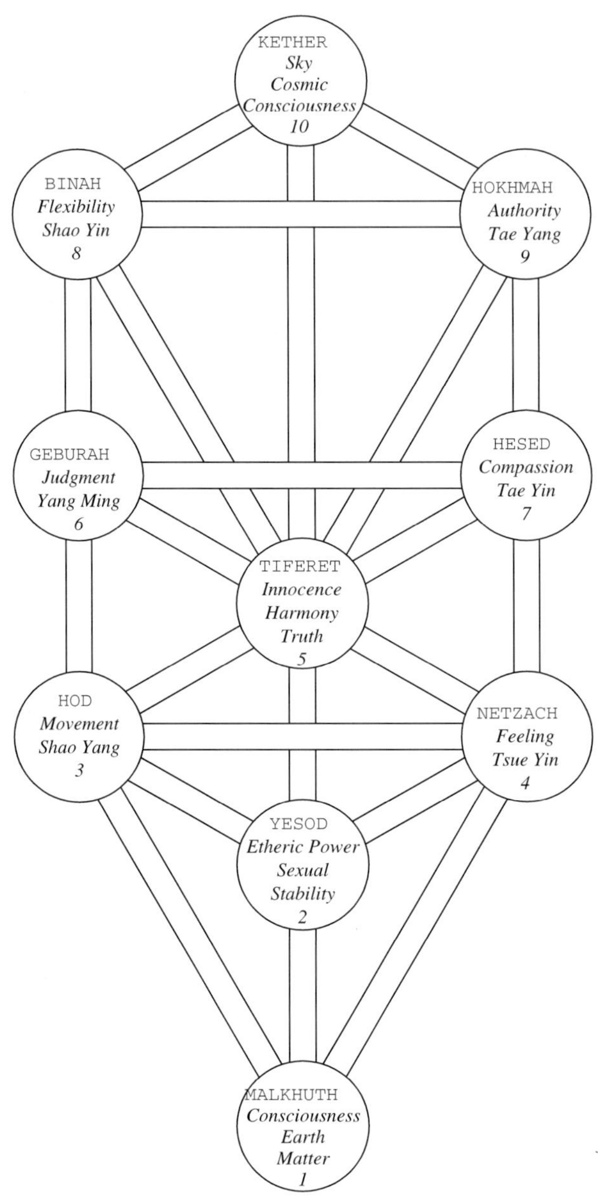

THE CHINESE TEMPERAMENTS AND THE SEFIROTIC TREE

Analogy between the Chinese Temperaments and the Sefirot

The Sefirotic Tree was originally designed as model showing the different initiatic states or pathways in the development of the human being. These states, or Sefira, could be divided into three main levels of understanding and development. These levels are given by the three horizontal axes of the Tree which each unite two Sefirot, one Yin and one Yang as shown in the preceding chart. The central axis of the Sefirotic tree (earth-moon-sun-cosmic source) makes the link between the two pillars to the left and right of this central axis.

Hod	Clever, adaptable	Netzach	Emotional, artistic
Geburah	Judgment, discipline	Hesed	Compassion, benevolence
Binah	Acceptance, intuition	Hokhmah	Decision, wisdom

We have in Chinese Medicine three main groups of psychological temperaments as well. These temperaments are associated by element two by two and anchored in the body by two internal organs. Chinese Temperaments are explained in detail Book III. The Chinese Temperaments are as follows:

Shao Yang:	Wood - Gall Bladder Fire -Triple Warmer	Fiery, Quick tempered
Tsue Yin:	Wood - Liver Fire - Pericardium	Nervous, Artistic
Shao Yin:	Fire - Heart Water - Kidneys	Sentimental, resigned
Tae Yang:	Water - Bladder Fire - Small Intestine	Authoritarian, Idealistic
Yang Ming:	Earth - Stomach Metal - Large Intestine	Cold minded, organizer

Tae Yin:	Metal - Lungs Earth - Spleen	Detached, tolerant

It may seem strange at first to make a correlation between the Chinese Temperaments and the Sefirotic Tree. It is like trying to find a correspondence between the speed of an ant or the pulse of a beaver with the movement of a star. The Chinese Temperaments with their anchor in the internal organs of the body seem to represent such a physical orientation, while the Sefirotic Tree seems to represent such a divine structure. But actually it does help to find a link, earth to sky, in order to understand how we can integrate our actions and reactions in the different levels of our lives.

Why are we sick? Why do we some people somatize through an organ of the body when going through a certain pathway or initiation in life which represents an emotional or spiritual crisis? Why can others pass through similar crises with ease?

The following analogy between the Chinese Temperaments and the Sefirot might shed some light on these questions.

1	Shao Yang	-	Hod	(Yang)
	Tsue Yin	-	Netzach	(Yin)
2	Yang Ming	-	Geburah	(Yang)
	Tae Yin	-	Hesed	(Yin)
3	Shao Yin	-	Binah	(Yin)
	Tae Yang	-	Hokhmah	(Yang)

We all have the six aspects of the Chinese Temperaments in us, like we have access to all of the qualities of the Sefirotic Tree. One or two aspects usually predominate, however, creating a strong disposition toward one of the Temperaments in each person.

When we are going through a certain initiation or pathway it helps to know with which Temperament we resonate. Our Temperament will describe which emotional tendencies and perhaps even which organs of the body the spiritual level can use to incarnate. Our biological and psychological characteristics, whether we have strong or weak organs or emotions, would determine the degree of somatization as we pass through a Sefira. This is where vitality, emotion, and clarity of the mental are linked with spiritual initiation.

The Chinese Temperaments and the Sefirot

1 A. Shao Yang - Hod (Yang)

The Shao Yang temperament is anchored on the wood and fire elements, corresponding to the gall bladder and the Triple Warmer (general energy) in the body. This association, fire/wood, makes the body, mind and emotions "burn" quickly. A Shao Yang person, therefore, is hyperactive, restless, agitated, always moving, and quick tempered.

These qualities also correspond to the qualities of the Sefira, Hod, which has a masculine yang aspect and a mercurial energy. Hod represents the ability to quickly process information just as the agile minded Shao Yang can do.

1 B. Tsue Yin - Netzach

Tsue Yin is a temperament based on the fire and wood elements in the Yin aspect which are anchored organically on the liver and pericardium (linked with sexual energy). A Tsue Yin person will enjoy beauty and be artistic, creative and imaginative. Emotionally, he or she will display a tendency to be nervous. The fire of Tsue Yin usually burns too fast, especially in relationships.

The Sefira Netzach represents the Beautiful Lady, full of virtue and joy, artistic and playful. But Netzach creates love through emotion in order to transform it into a higher purpose.

The Chinese Temperaments reveal the physical cause of emotional tendencies, whether one expresses strong emotion or not and whether one is active or passive. These factors all help to determine psychological behavior.

For example, in the Tsue Yin temperament, the element wood of the liver will produce creativity and ideas while the fire of the pericardium will determine the strength or weakness of the libido.

Netzach is the synonym of the higher level of Tsue Yin. Netah will translate the Tsue Yin qualities into an initiatic pathway.

2 A Yang Ming/ Geburah

The Yang Ming temperament is based on the earth and metal element supported by the stomach and large intestine. It is obvious that earth and metal will not have such an immediate and active interaction as the wood and fire interactions in the Shao Yang and Tsue Yin temperaments. It follows from the elements which compose Yang Ming that this temperament will more cold minded and not so disturbed by emotion as are the wood and fire temperaments. Yang Ming is objective, efficient, very respectful of the law and duty, strict or severe and an inflexible judge.

Likewise, Geburah, the Divine Warrior, respecter of duty and of law, also represents discipline and severity. Here again, the Sefira, Geburah, represents on a higher initiatic level the same qualities as the Yang Ming temperament.

2 B Tae Yin - Hesed

Tae Yin is based on earth and metal in the Yin aspect, anchored in the body to the spleen and the lungs. Tae Yin is quiet, accepting and compassionate. The detached attitude of Tae Yin seems to offer a tolerance to all. Tae Yin people are still and meditative, content with simplicity. They can "go with the flow" of life.

Hesed also represents compassion, kindness, mercy and human greatness (such as the Buddha-like Tae Yin ability to find contentment in simplicity and to remain meditative and still). Tae Yin is rooted in this simplicity through the elements earth and metal in the body. Hesed, as a spiritual quality, pushes one to this simplicity.

3 A Shao Yin - Binah

Shao Yin is a Yin temperament based on fire and water, supported by the heart and the kidneys in the body. Fire and water are two challenging elements to work with, because the fire brings passion, but the water instantly "puts out" the passion. The Shao Yin feels explosive inside, but the water element makes the Shao Yin person afraid to express passion, afraid to be open. This person, though he or she may hold everything inside, is extremely sensitive.

The Sefira, Binah, represents the transcendant aspect of the Shao Yin. If, through spiritual initiation, the Shao Yin could transcend the inner blocks to the expression of their passion and love, they would resemble the sensitive Binah, Mother Nature, the Divine Heart of intuition and acceptance of self and others with no fear to open the soul to life.

3 B Tae Yang - Hokhmah

Tae Yang consists of water and fire in the yang aspect supported by the small intestine and the bladder. The small intestine corresponds to the hara area of the body and the bladder meridian runs mainly along both sides of the spine, like a subtle energy structure running along the back. If the bladder energy is tight, this can give rigidity to the physical behavior.

With a straight back, the Tae Yang can resemble and behave with the rigidity of the archetypal military general and often this temperament does like to give orders and to control self and others. The Tae Yang is passionate, but, like the Shao Yin, the water aspect cools this passion, so it is not easily expressed. The Tae Yang is idealistic and willing to sacrifice for his or her ideal.

Hokhmah represents the Divine will power, discipline, and decision which are the higher qualities of the Tae Yang in the "military commander" aspect. Hokhmah can help the Tae Yang to transcend the earthly expression of decision-maker, commander into a higher representative of the Divine Will, whose very presence commands respect.

Even if each of us has a tendency towards one temperament because of our specific organic structure, we all experience parts of each temperament during the course of a lifetime. Family members and different partners in life will force us to understand some of the temperaments that are hidden to us, even if cyclically we return to our natural essence and innate behavior.

For example, a fiery, quick tempered and spontaneous Shao Yang person, anchored in his body through the gall bladder and Triple Warmer energies may be put in a position during his life where he is forced to experience the sentimental resignation of a Shao Yin temperament, which is based on the heart and kidneys. If the heart and kidney energy of the Shao Yang is strong organically, however, he will not play the inhibited, sensitive Shao Yin for long.

A Tae Yin person will not be hurt deeply or organically by the hurricanes and earthquakes of life because he or she is quiet inside, able to go with the flow. A Shao Yang person in the same situations will react so fast and with so much passion that the gall bladder will be strongly affected.

All of the spiritual initiations and lessons coming from the higher spheres which belong to the Sefirotic structure come into your being through the organic qualities you are made of (including whether you have strong or weak organs at birth). These organic qualities filter your emotional responses and understanding in life.

As you incarnate any of the Sefira or their pathways it is important to know your temperament qualities and your organic support. A Yang temperament and a Yin temperament will respond to and be affected by each Sefira's lessons very differently.

The Temperament and Sefirot correspondences are not restrictive. Of course we can incarnate into one lifetime any of the Sefirot qualities through any of the Temperaments. But knowing the correspondence between the Tree of Life and the Temperaments can offer help when we are going through difficult initiations.

If our current challenges are coming through Hod, we know that we must consolidate the gall bladder/Triple Warmer energy in the body. Help on the physical level through acupuncture or chi movement could aid the easy integration into the physical body of spiritual lessons of Hod. This way the spiritual initiations of the Sefirotic tree could be truly incarnated.

The essential is to know yourself. Know your organic, emotional and psychological strengths and weaknesses as described by the Chinese Temperaments. Know where you are on your life's pathway or spiritual pathway as described by the Sefirotic Tree and know where you are going.

When you understand these basic questions, who you are, of what you are made, where you are and where you are going, you will understand and accept why you behave and react as you do. This will end inner conflict and open you to the spiritual possibilities that you can incarnate into your life.

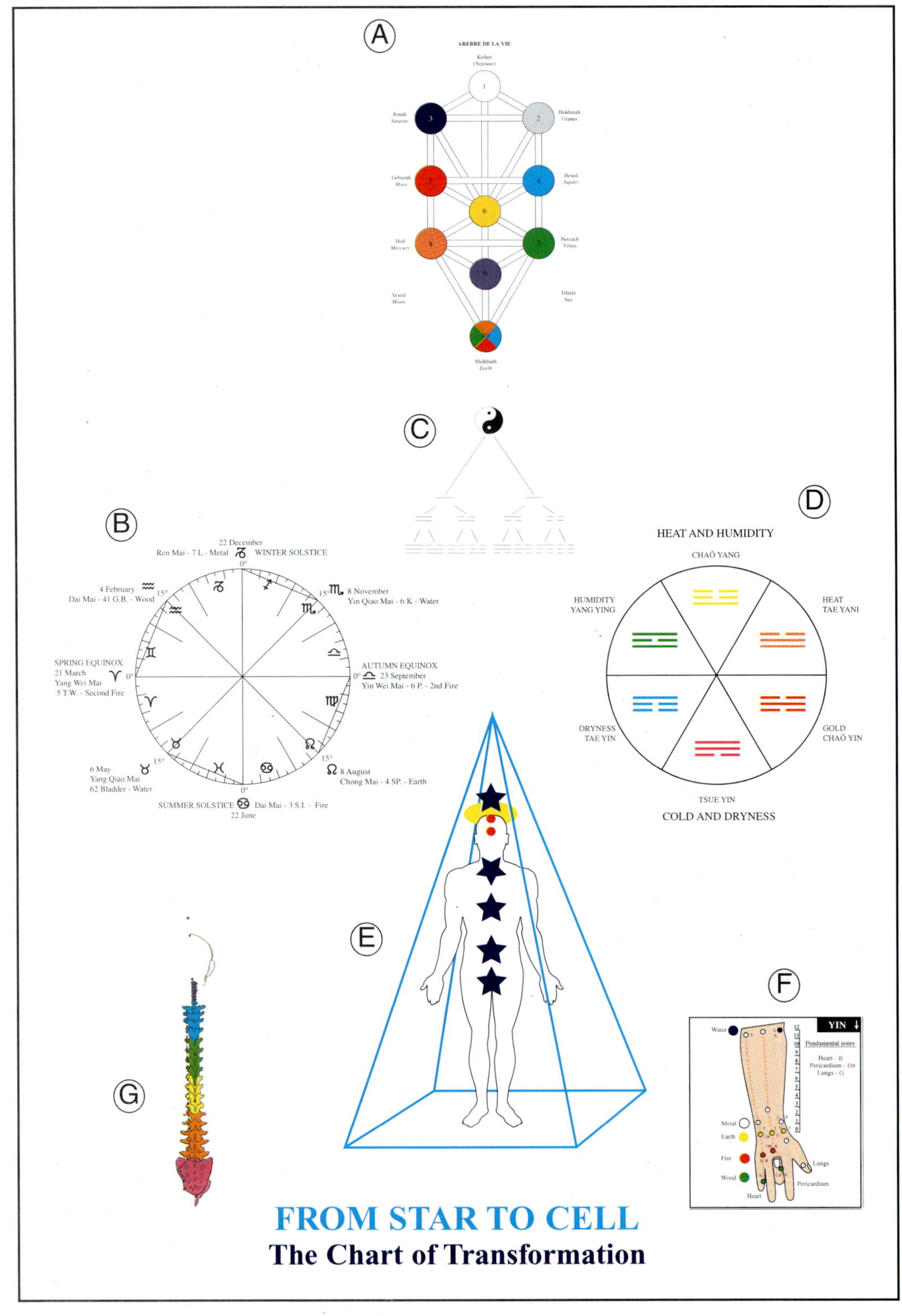

FROM STAR TO CELL
The Chart of Transformation

The Chart of Transformation

A. The Ten Sefirot of the Tree of Life were orginally the subtle blueprints of the planets before they became solid and physical.

B. These planetary subtle bodies are composed of cosmic chi. This energy, the cosmic chi, is carried to earth through the eight directions during the eight dates in the Zodiac where strong cosmic energy is manifested on earth.

C. The diagram of the Tao and the I Ching (which is also like the diagram of Kototama that corresponds to the Seventeen Secret Steps of creation) shows the necessary invisible states through which cosmic energy can manifest.

D. The cosmic energy is then transformed through what is called in Chinese Energy the Six Entities: Shao Yin, Tae Yang, Shao Yang, Tsue Yin, Tae Yin, Yang Ming. These entities also describe human psychological temperament. They diffuse and filter energy through the Five Shen, which are the emotional and spiritual correspondents of the five elements.[20]

E. The cosmic energy is then translated by the chakras to the physical body through the three "media" systems, the blood, the nervous and the meridian system. [21]

F. Cosmic energy then reaches the internal organs through the acupuncture points.

G. The final reception of this cosmic energy is integrated at the level of the cells and the DNA, including the most concentrated part of anatomy, the skeleton which remains after death as the last witness of the spirit on earth. Here is the final reception of energy, sky to earth by the human body.

Consciousness, according to each person's individual level of awareness, can work to assist any stage in this integration of cosmic energy into the human body.

Conclusion

From the Star to Acupuncture Point
The Chart of Transformation

Originally the Ten Sefirot were the etheric project of the planets from our solar system. From "The Source", cosmic energy, universal chi is transformed into different forms of density through the "Rays of Light" coming from the planets and stars into the Eight Directions, and then into a lower vibrational rate through "The Seventeen Secret Steps" which compose the I Ching Structure and finally into the DNA density. This integration of cosmic energy into the DNA of the human being is illustrated by the chart of transformation on page 108. As Madame Blavatsky teaches in The Cosmic Doctrine, "The invisible world duplicates its virtual structure into the physical world. This is a cosmic law."

"Each side of the pyramid is tuned to the musical mode which corresponds to its direction"

ADDENDUM

The Mystical Axis
The Ancient Brain as the "New Age" Liver

I include a special mention about liver problems because they are very common today. The source of liver imbalance is difficult to detect because this organ functions on many different levels.

The liver is linked with the element wood. Wood is linked with the "Tree of Life" of the human being. The liver, cut longitudinally reveals the shape of a tree. The essence, wood, makes the liver a link between the spiritual and the physical, just as a tree has its roots in the earth and its branches in the sky.

Many people present a liver imbalance through a gall bladder problem. They try many remedies, diets, etc. and still the problem remains unchanged. There are two reasons for this. The first is that the liver is the center of the Mystical Axis, which is an energy arriving through the Crown, going through the liver and then going out through the sexual organs in a right angle back to the universe. When everything is flowing well, the energy does not stop in any one of the three places. When there is an imbalance, energy can be stuck in the head, in the liver or in the sexual organs, creating imbalance. This Mystical Axis works with spiritual awareness. If we do not capture the spiritual information, it will be difficult to heal these three levels of the wood imbalance and specifically the liver.

The second reason for the difficulty in healing a liver imbalance is that, according to Rudolf Steiner, the liver was the ancient brain before our actual brain was developed. As the master of the organs of the body, it was a strong center for sensing vibration. This is related to the epoch when human beings, in early Lemurian times, had a sensitive body, a 'body of sensitivity' which predated the actual astral body. The liver functioned then almost like a brain.

Today the mental is extremely developed. When people, perhaps arriving at middle age, begin to give up on their social aims and purpose and drive to complete projects in the present, they delegate unconsciously these thoughts to the liver. The liver is then left carrying all of this unfinished business of the brain. This leaves it overcharged with too much energy.

Many people today who are on a spiritual path may have these problems because the spiritual quest sometimes takes one out of a strong focus in the present. They look to the past or future. As long as they have difficulty being in the present, they will find it impossible to be grounded like their "Tree of Life" and can develop a yang deficiency in the wood element of the body.

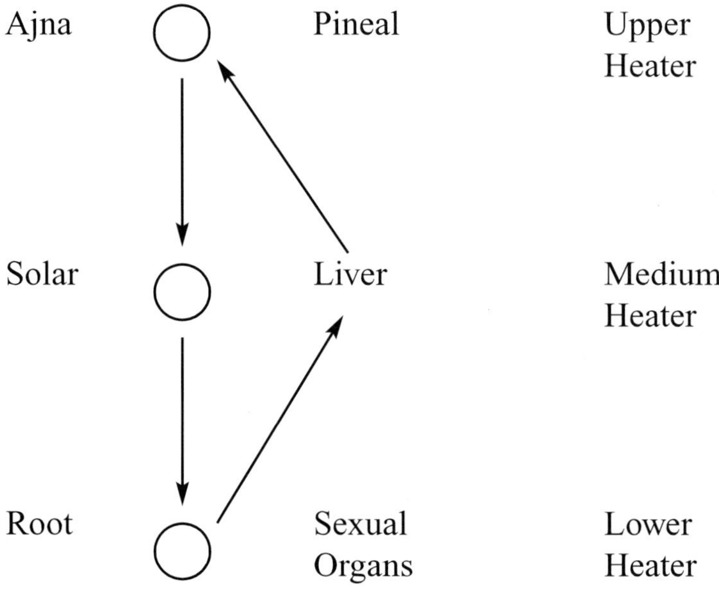

The Three Heaters of the Body
Mystical Axis

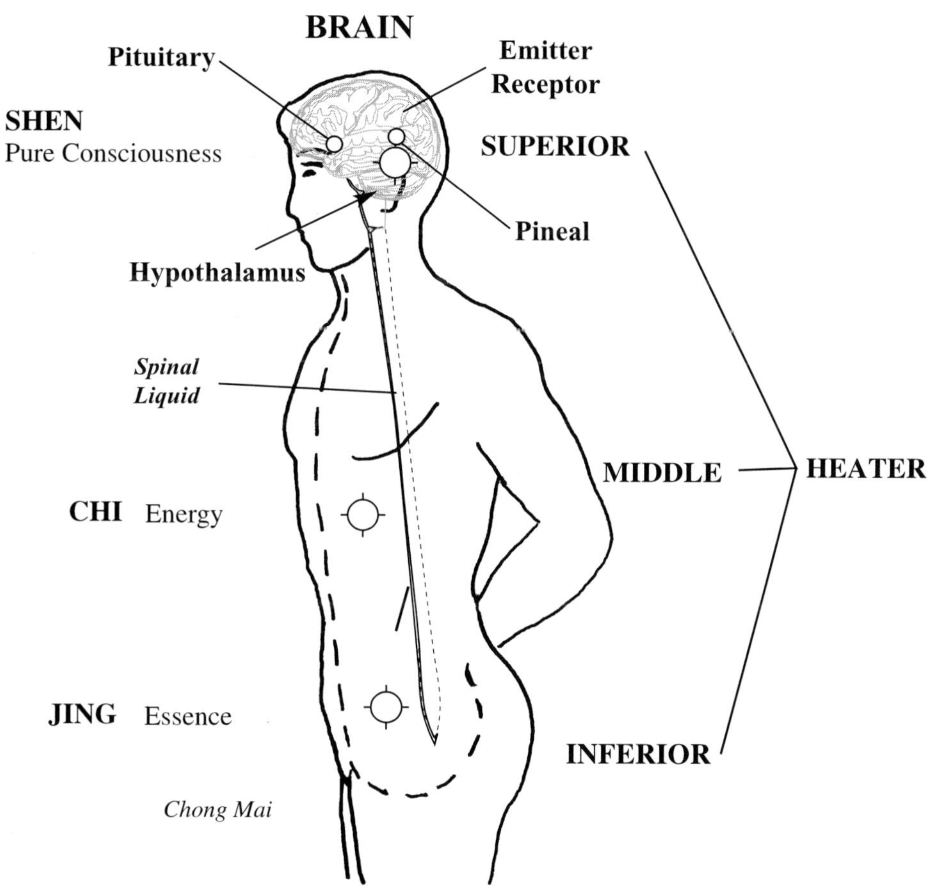

TRANSMUTATION
OF THE CHI IN THE 3 HEATERS

Footnotes

1 In the future we will be healing with the eyes. This possibility represents a new creode, another extremely fine level of creation and realization. Something will change in the human DNA code which will allow us to heal with the eyes. The human being is in mutation and transformation all of the time. When human consciousness reaches the level of what the eyes can do and what they really see, we will be able to use our eyes as a lazer to heal as masters or gurus can sometimes do when offering darshan to their disciples.

2 Overtones are discussed in Book I of this series: *The Role of Music in the Twenty-First Century.*

3 Sheldrake, Rupert, Une Nouvelle Science de la Vie, Monaco: *Editions de Rocher, 1985, (1981 Rupert Sheldrake).*

4 This concept of "stuck subtle body structure" is explained in detail in Book II: *Raising Human Frequencies, The Way of Chi and the Subtle Bodies.*

5 See Book II, *Raising Human Frequencies*, for the specific Tao Yin Fa techniques.

6 Book I, *The Role of Music in the Twenty-First Century*, discusses the particular quality and energetic influence of each musical interval.

7 Sternheimer, Joel *Compte-rendu de L'Academie des Sciences de Janvier,* 1983. *"La Musique des Particules Elementaire"* (The Music of the Elementary Particles). In his Brevette accepted by CNRS, (National Center for Scientific Research in Paris), physicist Joel Sternheimer offers his discovery that to each atomic particle (electron, lambda, sigma, etc.) there corresponds a frequency which is inversely proportional to its mass. According to Sternheimer, the frequency of the electron spin is close to the frequency A 440.

8 For those who do not know the Chinese Acupuncture pulses, they are introduced in Book III of this series, *Sound and Acupuncture* and can be found in any Acupuncture textbook.

9 The pitch of each season, according to Chinese Five Element Theory is A for Spring, C for Summer, G for Autumn, and D for winter, F for Indian Summer.

10 Tama-Do means "Way of the Soul".

11 If you would like more background in Chinese Medicine and the acupuncture meridian system, please refer to Book III in this series, *Sound and Acupuncture.*

12 For more information about musical intervals, see Book I of this series, *The Role of Music in the Twenty-First Century.*

13 The health of the physical body depends upon the health and vitality of the subtle bodies as explained in Book II.

14 Sternheimer, Joel, *La Musique des Particules Elementaire.* Physicist Joel Sternheimer has found that the frequency of the electron spin corresponds closely to the frequency A 440.

15 I will write about this in a future book entitled, *Sound Reflexology: Ear, Foot and Eye.*

16 The musical modes are discussed in detail in Book I of this series, *The Role of Music in the Twenty-First Century.*

17 To purchase audio cassettes with the modes of the Musical Spine chart played on the piano, please contact Tama-Do Press at the address at the end of the book.

18 There is a CD available, "Resonance of Ancestral Memories," Fabien Maman,1996, which uses the musical sequence and instruments for healing in the subtle bodies. Please contact Tama-Do Press at the address at the end of this book for more information.

19 The best quintessences I have found for this purpose are created by Patricia Janus of France. To order, contact Tama-Do Press at the address given at the end of this book.

20 The Six Entities and the Five Shen are explained in Book III. The Chart of Transformation will best be understood by those who have read the three previous books in this series.

21 The three media systems are described in Book II.

About the Author

Fabien Maman is a French musician, composer, acupuncturist, bioenergetician and martial artist. As a musician/composer, he performed many of his original compositions with his quintet in the great concert halls of the world, including Carnegie Hall, the Berlin Philharmonic, the Tokyo Opera and the Paris Olympia.

After an introduction to acupuncture during a musical tour in Japan, he put his performance career on hold in order to study acupuncture with Boris de Bardo in Paris. He was also a student of Sensei Nakazono who first brought Kototama, Science of Pure Sound, to the West.

Fabien Maman became an acupuncturist in 1977 and then linked music and acupuncture by discovering the musical frequencies of the acupuncture shu points. He developed a system which uses tuning forks instead of acupuncture needles.

In 1981, Fabien began a one and a half year experiment with biologist Hélène Grimal of the University of Jussieu in Paris to study the effect of sound in human cells. During the following years, he created several systems of healing which draw on his research with energy, sound, color and movement.

In 1987, Fabien Maman founded The Academy of Sound, Color and Movement, which offers the essence of his research in a practical form. In addition to their studies, each season the Academy students perform a harmonizing concert tuned with the musical key, mode and energy of the season in order to bring performers and audience into resonance with the vibration of earth and cosmic energies.

Fabien lives in the South of France and teaches courses from the Academy throughout the world.

All of the Healing Acoustic Instruments introduced in this book
are made especially for the Academy of Sound, Color and Movement by
Woflgang Lörler

Tama-Dō Press

For further information about the work of Fabien Maman, including CDs, audio and video cassettes, and workshops, please contact:

The Academy of Sound, Color and Movement
2060 Las Flores Canyon
Malibu, CA 90265
800.615.3675
info@tama-do.com
www.tamado.com

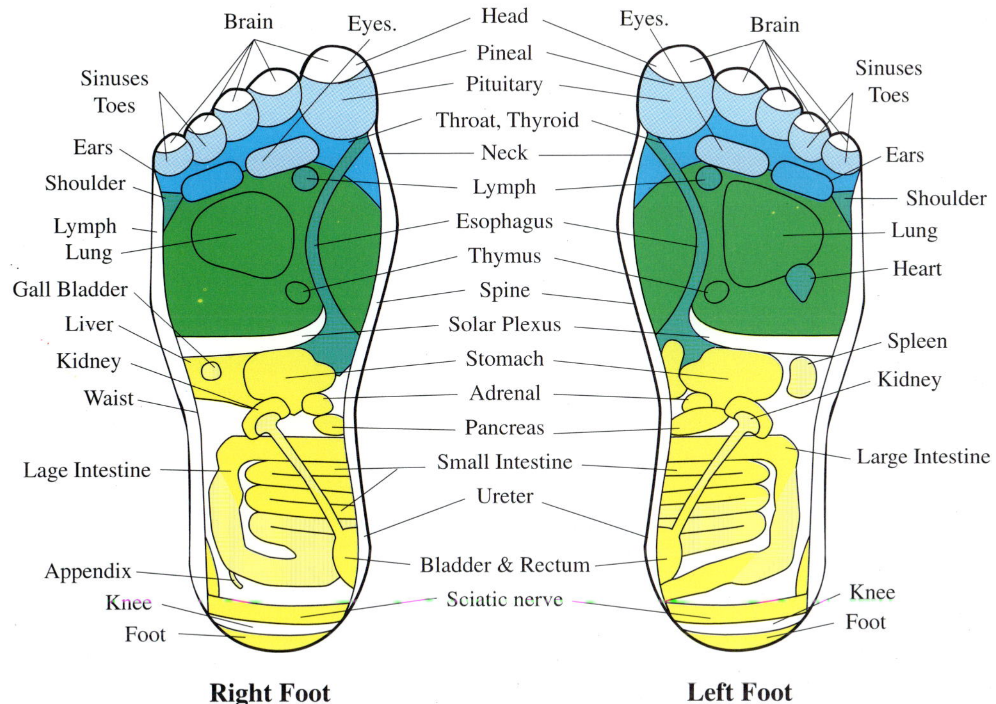

In the ear and the foot, the musical resonance of the reflex points works by zone; their organic correspondence is musically different from what they are along the acupuncture meridians.

USING FOOT AND EAR INTERVALS

1• When Stimulating Energy

FOOT		EAR
Bb	stomach	F
B	spleen	F#
G#	large intestine	D#
C	lungs	G
A	heart	E
D#	small intestine	Bb
G	liver	D
E	gall bladder	B
C	kidneys	G
C	bladder	G

2• When Sedating Energy

EAR		FOOT
F	stomach	A
F#	spleen	A#
D#	large intestine	G
G	lungs	B
E	heart	G#
Bb	small intestine	D
D	liver	F#
B	gall bladder	D#
G	kidneys	B
G	bladder	B

To stimulate, start the 5th interval in the foot and end in the ear. Sound first the tuning fork with the foot-pitch and then the other tuning fork with the ear-pitch.

To sedate, start the 3rd interval in the ear and end in the foot. Sound first the tuning fork with the ear-pitch and then the other tuning fork with the foot-pitch.

In both cases, the fundamental ear-pitch remains the same.